McDougal, Littell
SPELLING

Brown Level

Dolores Boylston Bohen
Assistant Superintendent
Fairfax County Public Schools
Fairfax County, Virginia

Mary Johanna Lincoln Huycke
Elementary Teacher and Reading Specialist
Fairfax County, Virginia

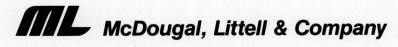 **McDougal, Littell & Company**

Evanston, Illinois
New York   Dallas   Sacramento   Raleigh

Objectives

- to teach the spelling of **words** as well as the spelling of sounds
- to stress the recognition of **structural** similarities as well as phonetic similarities
- to strengthen **associative** and **visual memory**
- to reinforce the **three modes of learning:** visual, auditory, and kinesthetic

Organization

Each lesson presents a word list that demonstrates one spelling pattern or generalization. The list is followed by three types of activities:

Practice the Words—three activities that require students to examine and write the words on the spelling list at least twice

Build Word Power—an activity that extends the application of words on the spelling list in a broader language arts context

Reach Out for New Words—two activities in which students work with new words that follow the spelling pattern

CONSULTANTS FOR THIS TEXT

Georgene G. Albert, Teacher, Pine Tree Independent School District, Longview, Texas
Olive L. Engebretson, Teacher, School District of Chetek, Chetek, Wisconsin
Ann B. Hackett, Teacher, Traverse City Area Public Schools, Traverse City, Michigan
David V. Johnson, Curriculum Specialist, Mount Diablo School District, Concord, California
Barbara E. Marthaler, Teacher, Millcreek Township School District, Erie, Pennsylvania
Joanne McDonald, Teacher, Portage Public Schools, Portage, Michigan
Evelyn J. Meredith, Teacher, District 208, Oneida, Illinois
Edith M. Olson, Teacher, Barron School District, Barron, Wisconsin
David E. Prince, Teacher, Irvine Unified School District, Irvine, California
Claire A. Stewart, Teacher, Jefferson Public Schools, Jefferson, Wisconsin
Jacqueline Wadlinger, Teacher, Durham County Schools, Durham, North Carolina
Elsa E. Woods, Principal, Durham County Schools, Durham, North Carolina

Acknowledgments
Marian Reiner: For "Secret Talk" from *A Word or Two with You* by Eve Merriam; copyright © 1981 by Eve Merriam, all rights reserved. Marian Reiner: for "Think of Tree" from *I Thought I Heard the City* by Lilian Moore; copyright © 1969 by Lilian Moore, all rights reserved.

ISBN 0-8123-5388-9

Copyright © 1990 by McDougal, Littell & Company
Box 1667, Evanston, Illinois 60204
All rights reserved. Printed in the United States of America

90 91 92 93 / 15 14 13 12 11 10 9 8 7 6 5 4 3 2

Contents

A Writer's Journal

Spelling Is for Writing

Imagine that you are drawing a picture of your friend. You want to show just what your friend looks like. Now imagine that you are writing about that friend. You want to use certain words in your description. But wait! What will happen if you cannot spell any of those words?

You learn to spell in order to write. Writing is something you do often. This book will help you improve both your spelling and your writing. The more you practice both skills, the better speller and writer you will become.

One way to practice writing is to keep a journal. A journal is a notebook where you write your ideas, feelings—anything at all.

Start to keep a journal today. Write in it often. Sometimes you may write a few lines. At other times you may fill several pages. Here are some ways to use your journal.

- Write what you think or feel.
- Remember special times in your life.
- Describe how something looks or sounds.
- Tell about a favorite story or poem.

Spelling and Your Journal

When you write in your journal, you may want to use words you cannot spell. Do not stop writing. Write the words as you think they should be spelled. Later, look up the correct spelling in the dictionary. Keep a personal word list of these words. Then, whenever you need to write them again, just check your list.

Getting Started

If you need an idea for your first journal entry, start with one of these.

1. Today I imagined that . . .
2. You should see the _____ that I saw!

Building a Personal Word List

What Is a Personal Word List?

Your spelling book shows you how to spell many words. It also gives you information about how words in our language are spelled. In this way, the book helps you become a better writer. Sometimes, however, you will need to write a new word that you do not know how to spell. You can put this word on a special list called a personal word list. This is a list of words that *you* want to learn how to spell and use. This list is special because *you* choose the words you want to make your own.

Words for your personal list can come from anywhere—your writing, your reading, or your conversations. You also might discover words for your list in these other places:

- your journal entries
- your other subjects
- stories and poems you write
- newspapers and magazines

How to Keep a Personal Word List

Write your personal words in a special place. This might be in the back of your journal or in a special notebook. Be sure to keep your list handy. That way, you can add words and look at the list easily.

As you collect the words, check them carefully. Notice the kinds of spelling mistakes you make. Think about the words. Do any of them look like words you know how to spell?

Making Words Your Own

Making a word your own means making it one you can use in your writing. You will need to know its meaning and correct spelling. A dictionary can help you. Then you will want to learn to spell the word. The steps on page 7 show one way you might use to learn to spell words.

How to Spell a Word

Each week you will be learning to spell a new list of words. You will also be learning words from your personal list. You will need a system—or strategy—for studying these words. One way to learn to spell a word is explained below. You can use it as you prepare for your weekly spelling test and as you learn to spell words on your personal list.

1. Look at the word.

2. Say the word.

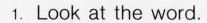

3. Spell the word aloud.

4. Copy the word.

5. Picture the word in your mind.

6. Cover the word and write it.

Check for mistakes.
If you have made a mistake,
repeat steps 1 to 6.

mile	*mile*
lake	*lake*
race	*race*
place	*place*
hose	*hose*
cage	*cage*
size	*size*
prize	*prize*
stone	*stone*
paste	*paste*
since	*since*
once	*once*
more	*more*
none	*none*
gone	*gone*

1. What is the last letter you see in the word **mile**? ____

2. What is the last letter you hear in the word **mile**? ____

3. The words in the first column end with a letter that cannot be heard. What is that letter? ____

Many words end with a final silent **e**.

A Print the spelling word that fits in the shapes and rhymes with the clue word.

1. space   `place`

2. size

3. taste

4. pose

5. done

6. store

7. prince

8. bone

9. face

10. file

11. prize

12. rage

13. bake

9

B Find the misspelled word in each group. Then write the word correctly.

1. size

   lake

   plase

   _____

   _ _ _ _ _ _ _ _ _

   _____

2. wonce

   stone

   mile

   _____

   _ _ _ _ _ _ _ _ _

   _____

3. hose

   more

   caje

   _____

   _ _ _ _ _ _ _ _ _

   _____

C Use each clue to find a spelling word that fits the boxes. Write the words.

1. what a winner gets

2. a running contest

3. for watering grass

4. a rock

5. opposite of **less**

   _____

   _ _ _ _ _ _ _ _ _

Write the word you see in the colored boxes.   _____

6. how big a thing is

7. a long distance

8. not any

9. one time

10. no longer here

   _____

   _ _ _ _ _ _ _ _ _

Write the word you see in the colored boxes.   _____

Build Word Power

Writing

Choose a spelling word. Write an acrostic poem about your word.

RACE
Run fast to stay
ahead until you
come to the
end.

CAGE
Closed inside
a tiger was
growling and
eating his food.

Let the spelling word be the <u>title</u> of your poem.
Begin each line with a letter of the spelling word.
Start the poem with a capital letter. End it with a period.

New Words   vase   smoke   therefore   tire
          else   price   picture   breeze

Reach Out for New Words

A Find the eight new silent **e** words in this puzzle. Circle each word.
Then write it on the line. Some words may overlap.

1. _____

2. _____

3. _____

4. _____

5. _____

6. _____

7. _____

8. _____

Proofreading

B Cross out each misspelled word. Write it correctly.

1. The tiar is flat. Therefor, we must walk.

_____   _____

_____   _____

2. The breeze is blowing smoak at me.

_____

_____

3. What is the prise of this flower vaes?

_____   _____

_____   _____

12

boat	*boat*
coat	*coat*
goat	*goat*
float	*float*
road	*road*
load	*load*
toad	*toad*
toast	*toast*
oak	*oak*
soak	*soak*
soap	*soap*
coach	*coach*
throat	*throat*
coast	*coast*
oats	*oats*

1. The letters **a**, **e**, **i**, **o**, and **u** are vowels. What two vowels are in each word? ____ ____
2. Which one of the two vowels do you hear when you say these words? ____

Some vowels are paired to spell one sound.
Many words are spelled with the vowels **oa**.

boat   goat   road   toad   oak   soap   throat   oats

coat   float   load   toast   soak   coach   coast

Practice the Words

A Use each clue to find a spelling word that fits in the puzzle.

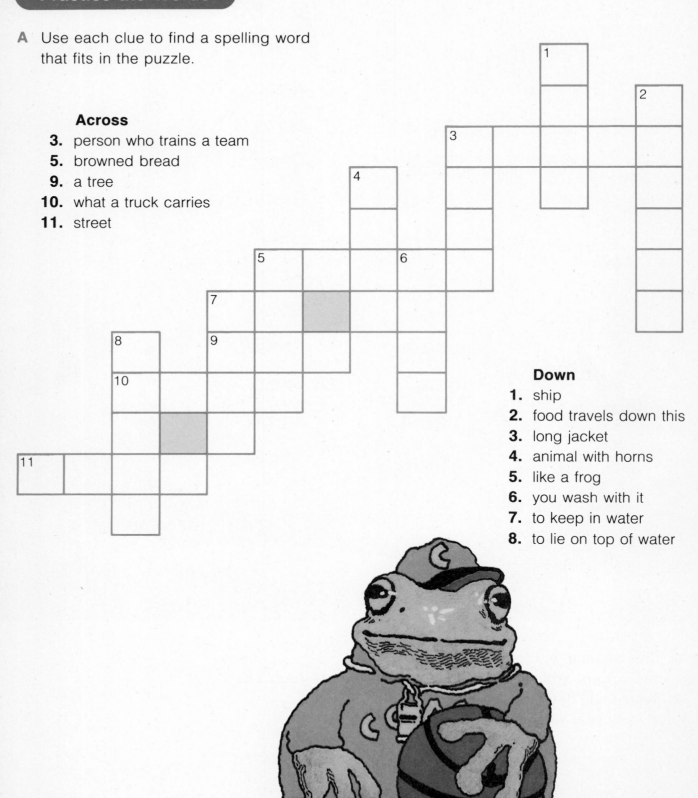

Across

3. person who trains a team
5. browned bread
9. a tree
10. what a truck carries
11. street

Down

1. ship
2. food travels down this
3. long jacket
4. animal with horns
5. like a frog
6. you wash with it
7. to keep in water
8. to lie on top of water

14

B Answer each question with spelling words.

1. Which five words have the letter **s**?

_____ _____ _____

- - - - - - - - - - - -   - - - - - - - - - - - -   - - - - - - - - - - - -

_____ _____ _____

- - - - - - - - - - - -

_____ _____

2. Which three words have the letter **d**?

_____ _____ _____

- - - - - - - - - - - -   - - - - - - - - - - - -   - - - - - - - - - - - -

_____ _____ _____

3. Which four-letter words end with the letter **t**?

_____ _____ _____

- - - - - - - - - - - -   - - - - - - - - - - - -   - - - - - - - - - - - -

_____ _____

C Unscramble each group of letters to make a spelling word.

1. posa	_____	**9.** staot	_____
2. loaft	_____	**10.** oask	_____
3. otca	_____	**11.** dloa	_____
4. accho	_____	**12.** ako	_____
5. tago	_____	**13.** dota	_____
6. otba	_____	**14.** droa	_____
7. osta	_____	**15.** scoat	_____
8. rattoh	_____		

Build Word Power

Writing

Write some silly sentences. Use two or more **oa** words in each sentence. Circle those words. Use as many different spelling words as you can. Remember to start each sentence with a capital letter and end it with a period.

1. The (toad) ate (toast) under the (oak) tree.

2.

3.

4.

Reach Out for New Words

A The three words in each group below belong together.
Write the new **oa** word that goes with each word group.

1. wood, oil, coal, _____

2. bake, fry, broil, _____

3. juice, milk, tea, _____

4. earn, spend, save, _____

5. brag, gloat, cheer, _____

6. moan, cry, sob, _____

B Find the misspelled word in each group. Then write the word
correctly.

1. coat

baost

toast

oak

_____

_____

2. road

coco

boat

groan

_____

_____

3. goat

load

laon

float

_____

_____

4. coach

boast

soak

charcole

_____

_____

5. raost

toad

soap

toast

_____

_____

6. soap

float

groane

coach

_____

_____

<u>ou</u>t	*out*
ab<u>ou</u>t	*about*
c<u>ou</u>nt	*count*
f<u>ou</u>nd	*found*
gr<u>ou</u>nd	*ground*
r<u>ou</u>nd	*round*
ar<u>ou</u>nd	*around*
s<u>ou</u>nd	*sound*
l<u>ou</u>d	*loud*
cl<u>ou</u>d	*cloud*
m<u>ou</u>th	*mouth*
s<u>ou</u>th	*south*
h<u>ou</u>r	*hour*
h<u>ou</u>se	*house*
m<u>ou</u>se	*mouse*

What pair of vowels do you see in every word? ____ ____

Many words are spelled with the vowels **ou**.

18

Practice the Words

A Write the spelling words that complete these sentences.

1. Birds fly _____ for the winter.

2. A marching band plays very _____ music.

3. I hear the _____ of an airplane flying.

4. Dale wrote a story _____ horses.

5. My little brother can _____ from one to ten.

6. The sun was hidden behind a _____.

7. A baseball is _____, but a football is not.

8. I burned my _____ on some hot soup.

9. Kim took a sweater _____ of the drawer.

10. In the mile race, the girls ran _____ the track four times.

11. I _____ a dollar on the _____.

12. There are three bedrooms in our _____.

13. The football game starts in one _____.

out	found	around	cloud	hour
about	ground	sound	mouth	house
count	round	loud	south	mouse

B Complete each phrase with a spelling word.

1. not **in**, but _____

2. not **lost**, but _____

3. not **north**, but _____

4. not **square**, but _____

5. not the **sky**, but the _____

6. not **quiet**, but _____

7. not a **minute**, but an _____

8. not a **cat**, but a _____

C Print the spelling word that rhymes with the clue and fits in the shape.

1. shout

4. south

2. hound

5. proud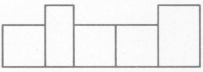

3. mount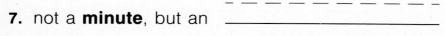

6. round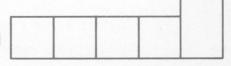

20

Follow the directions to change each clue word into two spelling words.

1. **hound** Change **h** to **s** to make

   Change **s** to **r** to make

2. **mount** Change **nt** to **th** to make

   Change **m** to **s** to make

3. **grouch** Change **ch** to **nd** to make

   Change **g** to **a** to make

4. **shout** Change **sh** to **ab** to make

   Take off **ab** to make

5. **proud** Change **pr** to **cl** to make

   Take off **c** to make

6. **mound** Change **nd** to **se** to make

   Change **m** to **h** to make

sound

New Words   outdoors   couch   blouse   mountain
                 scout   amount   fountain   flour

Reach Out for New Words

A Find the eight new **ou** words in this puzzle. Circle each word. Then write it on a line.

1. _____

2. _____

3. _____

4. _____

5. _____

6. _____

7. _____

8. _____

B Write the new **ou** word that matches each meaning.

1. shirt

_____

2. sofa

_____

3. not indoors

_____

4. how much

_____

5. a powder for baking

_____

6. very high hill

_____

7. stream of water

_____

8. to search for

_____

22

bed	+ s =	beds	*beds*
leg	+ s =	legs	*legs*
step	+ s =	steps	*steps*
flag	+ s =	flags	*flags*
clock	+ s =	clocks	*clocks*
fox	+ es =	foxes	*foxes*
box	+ es =	boxes	*boxes*
inch	+ es =	inches	*inches*
lunch	+ es =	lunches	*lunches*
dish	+ es =	dishes	*dishes*
wish	+ es =	wishes	*wishes*
brush	+ es =	brushes	*brushes*
bus	+ es =	buses	*buses*
glass	+ es =	glasses	*glasses*
class	+ es =	classes	*classes*

A word that names something is called a **noun**.
A noun that names <u>one</u> thing is a **singular** noun.
A noun that names <u>more than one</u> thing is a **plural** noun.

1. The nouns in the first column are singular nouns.

How many end with **x**? _____ with **ch**? _____ with **s**? _____ with **sh**? _____

2. The nouns in the second column are plural nouns.

What one letter has been added to some words? _____

What two letters have been added to other words? _____ _____

Make many nouns plural by adding **s**.
When a noun ends with **x**, **ch**, **s**, or **sh**, add **es** to make the plural form.

A Write the spelling words that complete these sentences.

1. Tom will wash the _____ after dinner.

2. My sister packed our _____ in brown bags.

3. Three _____ just left the station.

4. This belt is twenty _____ long.

5. Drink three _____ of milk each day.

6. We walked up the _____ to the next floor.

7. Two _____ were flying from the same pole.

8. My brother and I sleep in bunk _____ .

9. The school _____ were ten minutes fast.

10. The _____ had bushy red tails.

11. Mary packed the books in cardboard _____ .

12. All of the painter's _____ need cleaning.

13. A spider has eight _____ .

14. My sister _____ she had a puppy.

foxes	lunches	brushes	classes	steps
boxes	dishes	buses	beds	flags
inches	wishes	glasses	legs	clocks

B Look at each word. If it is spelled correctly, draw a ☺.
If it is misspelled, write the word correctly.

1. flages _____

2. glasses _____

3. foxes _____

4. steps _____

5. clases _____

6. inchs _____

7. buses _____

8. clockes _____

9. brushs _____

10. wishs _____

C Unscramble each group of letters to make a singular word. Then
write its plural form. The first word is done for you.

1. slags glass glasses

2. ofx _____ _____

3. deb _____ _____

4. huncl _____ _____

5. spet _____ _____

6. sub _____ _____

7. oxb _____ _____

8. hids _____ _____

9. elg _____ _____

10. scals _____ _____

foxes	lunches	brushes	classes	steps
boxes	dishes	buses	beds	flags
inches	wishes	glasses	legs	clocks

Build Word Power

Unscramble each group of words to make a sentence. The first
word has a capital letter. Put a period at the end of each sentence.
Circle each spelling word.

1. flags the at Look.

Look at the flags.

2. up Walk steps the.

3. lunch ate The foxes.

4. bed near The clock my is.

5. box The is tall inches six.

6. dishes Wash and glasses the the.

Search for new words!
Follow the directions below.

Reach Out for New Words

A Find the correct path through this maze. Words that add **es** to make the plural form are on the correct path. Write the seven words that are on the correct path.

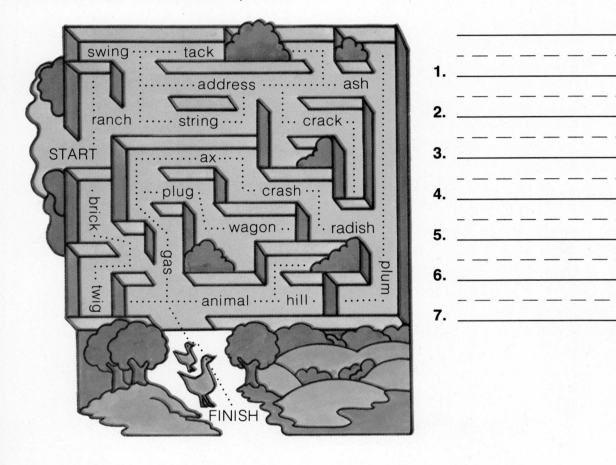

1. _____

2. _____

3. _____

4. _____

5. _____

6. _____

7. _____

B Write the plural form of each word that was on the correct path through the maze.

1. _____

2. _____

3. _____

4. _____

5. _____

6. _____

7. _____

t<u>oy</u>	toy<u>s</u>	*toys*
cowb<u>oy</u>	cowboy<u>s</u>	*cowboys*
d<u>ay</u>	day<u>s</u>	*days*
b<u>ay</u>	bay<u>s</u>	*bays*
r<u>ay</u>	ray<u>s</u>	*rays*
pl<u>ay</u>	play<u>s</u>	*plays*
tr<u>ay</u>	tray<u>s</u>	*trays*
runw<u>ay</u>	runway<u>s</u>	*runways*
bluej<u>ay</u>	bluejay<u>s</u>	*bluejays*
birthd<u>ay</u>	birthday<u>s</u>	*birthdays*
k<u>ey</u>	key<u>s</u>	*keys*
monk<u>ey</u>	monkey<u>s</u>	*monkeys*
turk<u>ey</u>	turkey<u>s</u>	*turkeys*
donk<u>ey</u>	donkey<u>s</u>	*donkeys*
vall<u>ey</u>	valley<u>s</u>	*valleys*

1. The nouns in the first column end with the letter _____.

2. Is the letter before each final **y** a vowel? _____

3. The nouns in the second column are plural.

   What letter has been added to form the plural? _____

> When a noun ends with **vowel + y**, add the letter **s** to form the plural.

Practice the Words

A Write the spelling words that complete these sentences.

1. The drama club gave two _____ plays _____ this year.

2. Airplanes land on _____.

3. Most _____ know how to ride horses.

4. Two _____ pulled the hay wagon.

5. My aunt raises geese and _____.

6. The map showed rivers, seas, and _____.

7. My mother works three _____ a week.

8. The _____ of the sun give us light.

9. Sue put her games and _____ away.

10. Put all the glasses on those _____.

11. Bob and Rosa's _____ are both in May.

12. Dad lost all the _____ to the house.

13. Low places between hills are called _____.

B Add the missing vowels to complete each word. Then write the plural form.

1. c__wb__y _____

2. b__rthd__y _____

3. m__nk__y _____

4. t__rk__y _____

5. r__nw__y _____

6. v__ll__y _____

Dictionary

Words in the dictionary are listed in **alphabetical order**.

a b c d e f g h i j k l m n o p q r s t u v w x y z

C Write each group of words in alphabetical order. When two or more words begin with the same letter, look at the second letter.

lamp
like
luck

1 _____

donkeys _____

bays _____

keys _____

days _____

bluejays _____

2 _____

turkeys _____

toys _____

runways _____

trays _____

rays _____

toys	bays	trays	birthdays	turkeys
cowboys	rays	runways	keys	donkeys
days	plays	bluejays	monkeys	valleys

Build Word Power

Writing

Read these ABC poems.

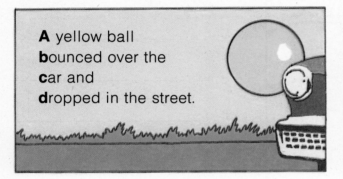

A yellow ball
bounced over the
car and
dropped in the street.

Kittens
like to
meow and
nap in the sunshine.

Use spelling words to write two of your own ABC poems. The beginning letters of the lines are in alphabetical order. You may start the first line with any letter.

1. _____

2. _____

Search for new words!
Follow the directions below.

Reach Out for New Words

A Look at the word in each space. Color the space red if the word ends in a **vowel + y**. Color the other spaces blue. Write the words from the red spaces on the lines.

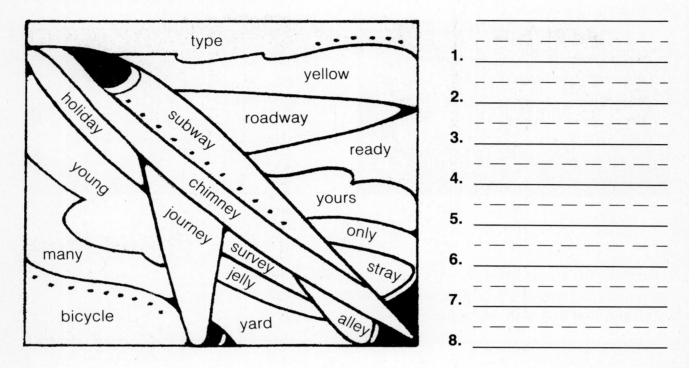

1. _____

2. _____

3. _____

4. _____

5. _____

6. _____

7. _____

8. _____

B Write the plural form of each new word.

1. _____   5. _____

2. _____   6. _____

3. _____   7. _____

4. _____   8. _____

fly	flies	*flies*
city	cities	*cities*
copy	copies	*copies*
baby	babies	*babies*
lady	ladies	*ladies*
pony	ponies	*ponies*
daisy	daisies	*daisies*
party	parties	*parties*
candy	candies	*candies*
cherry	cherries	*cherries*
bunny	bunnies	*bunnies*
puppy	puppies	*puppies*
penny	pennies	*pennies*
berry	berries	*berries*
butterfly	butterflies	*butterflies*

1. Each word in the first column ends with the letter _____.

2. The letters **a**, **e**, **i**, **o**, and **u** are called _____.
   The other letters of the alphabet are called **consonants**.

3. Do the words in the first column have
   a <u>consonant</u> or a <u>vowel</u> before the final **y**? _____

4. The nouns in the second column are plural.
   What are the last three letters of these words? __ __ __

To make the plural form of a noun that ends with **consonant + y**,
change the **y** to **i** and add **es**.

flies   babies   daisies   cherries   pennies
cities   ladies   parties   bunnies   berries
copies   ponies   candies   puppies   butterflies

Practice the Words

A Use each clue to find a spelling word that fits in the boxes.

1. little children

2. young dogs

3. large towns

4. birthday_____

5. cents

6. small fruits

7. bugs

8. women

9. writes again

10. chocolates

11. baby rabbits

What spelling word do you see
in the colored boxes?

34

Proofreading

B Cross out each misspelled word. Write the word correctly.

1. The butterflis landed on the daises.

    _____   _____

    _____   _____

2. We ate ice cream with beries at the partie.

    _____   _____

    _____   _____

3. The ponis brushed the flys off their backs.

    _____   _____

    _____   _____

4. The ladies bought cherrys at the fruit stand.

    _____

    _____

Dictionary

C Write each group of words in alphabetical order. When two or more
   words begin with the same letter, look at the second letter.

1 _____   2 _____

candies _____   pennies _____

babies _____   ponies _____

copies _____   ladies _____

cities _____   puppies _____

bunnies _____   parties _____

cherries _____   daisies _____

flies	babies	daisies	cherries	pennies
cities	ladies	parties	bunnies	berries
copies	ponies	candies	puppies	butterflies

Build Word Power

Follow the directions for changing each clue word into the singular form of a spelling word. Write each word. Then write the plural form of the word.

	Clue	Change	Singular	Plural
1.	buddy	**dd** to **nn**	bunny	bunnies
2.	parts	**s** to **y**		
3.	pity	**p** to **c**		
4.	lazy	**z** to **d**		
5.	pond	**d** to **y**		
6.	peppy	**pp** to **nn**		
7.	belly	**ll** to **rr**		
8.	carry	**rr** to **nd**		
9.	puffy	**ff** to **pp**		
10.	body	**od** to **ab**		
11.	fry	**r** to **l**		
12.	cone	**ne** to **py**		
13.	dairy	**r** to **s**		
14.	merry	**m** to **ch**		

Reach Out for New Words

A Words are printed in three directions in this puzzle. → ↓ ↘ Find and circle nine **consonant + y** words. Write each word.

```
b  o  d  y  h  b  c
a  f  e  r  r  y  o
k  f  a  j  d  g  m
e  a  r  m  y  m  p
r  s  p  y  i  k  a
y  d  u  t  y  l  n
c  l  e  n  e  m  y
```

1. _____

2. _____

3. _____

4. _____

5. _____

6. _____

7. _____

8. _____

9. _____

B Write the plural form of each new word.

1. _____

2. _____

3. _____

4. _____

5. _____

6. _____

7. _____

8. _____

9. _____

man	men	*men*
woman	women	*women*
foot	feet	*feet*
tooth	teeth	*teeth*
mouse	mice	*mice*
deer	deer	*deer*
sheep	sheep	*sheep*
elf	elves	*elves*
calf	calves	*calves*
wolf	wolves	*wolves*
shelf	shelves	*shelves*
leaf	leaves	*leaves*
loaf	loaves	*loaves*
wife	wives	*wives*
knife	knives	*knives*

1. How many words change their spelling to make the plural form? _____

2. How many plural words are the same as the singular words? _____

3. How many words change **f** or **fe** to **v** and add **es** to make the plural form? _____

Some nouns make the plural form in an unusual way.
Sometimes a new word is used.
Sometimes the same word is used for both the singular and plural forms.
Some nouns that end with **f** or **fe** change the **f** or **fe** to **v** and
    add **es** to make the plural form.

A Write the singular words in alphabetical order in the first column.
Then complete the chart.

Singular Form	Plural Form	How many letters are the same?
1. calf	calves	3
2.		
3.		
4.		
5.		
6.		
7.		
8.		
9.		
10.		
11.		
12.		
13.		
14.		
15.		

B Write the spelling word that fits each clue.

1. what books are kept on _____

2. things that grow on trees _____

3. married women _____

4. used for cutting _____

5. bread comes in these _____

6. small people in folk tales _____

7. baby cows _____

8. wild animals that howl _____

C Add the missing letters to make plural words.

1. m __ c __   5. s __ e __ p

2. f __ e __   6. d __ e __

3. w __ m __ n   7. t __ e __ h

4. m __ n   8. w __ l __ e __

Build Word Power

Each number in this code stands for one letter of the alphabet.
Decode each word and write it.

One Friday evening, Mr. Wilson and his ___ ___ ___ ___ baked
8 13 20 3

thirteen ___ ___ ___ ___ ___ ___ of their famous bread to sell at the town
5 17 2 7 3 4

fair. They stored the bread on their kitchen ___ ___ ___ ___ ___ ___ ___ .
4 6 3 5 7 3 4

Later that night the Wilsons heard ___ ___ ___ ___ ___ ___
5 3 2 7 3 4

rustling outside their bedroom window. At first they thought

___ ___ ___ ___ ___ ___ were after their ___ ___ ___ ___ ___ or
8 17 5 7 3 4   4 6 3 3 11

___ ___ ___ ___ ___ ___ . Then a window opened. Two
19 2 5 7 3 4

___ ___ ___ ___ ___ climbed in, wearing soft slippers on their
8 17 1 3 24

___ ___ ___ ___ . As quietly as ___ ___ ___ ___ ___ the Wilsons followed
20 3 3 15   3 5 7 3 4

them toward the kitchen. There they were, eating the loaves of bread!

1. _____

2. _____

3. _____

4. _____

5. _____

6. _____

7. _____

8. _____

9. _____

10. _____

New Words   oxen   lives   geese   halves
thieves   children   yourselves

Reach Out for New Words

A Words are printed in three directions in this puzzle. → ↓ ↘ Find the singular form of each new word. Circle it in the puzzle. Then write it on the line.

```
y  h  f  j  d  n  k  p
g  o  o  s  e  p  l  s
m  x  u  f  q  l  g  q
c  v  g  r  k  i  y  v
c  w  d  t  s  f  h  n
t  h  i  e  f  e  a  r
z  h  b  c  h  i  l  d
b  x  r  j  s  m  f  f
```

1. _____

2. _____

3. _____

4. _____

5. _____

6. _____

7. _____

Proofreading

B Cross out each misspelled word. Write the word correctly.

1. The childrun divided the cake into two haves.

   _____   _____

2. Two thiefs stole our gooses.

   _____   _____

3. These oxes have spent their whole lifes on our farm.

   _____   _____

4. Did you build this cabin yourselfs?

   _____

1.
place
prize
once

2.
boat
coat
road

3.
out
about
sound

4.

bed	beds
dish	dishes
glass	glasses

5.

toy	toys
birthday	birthdays
key	keys

6.

city	cities
party	parties
penny	pennies

7.

woman	women
wolf	wolves
knife	knives

A Look at the first pair of words in each row. In what way do these words go together? Write a spelling word that makes the second pair of words go together in the same way as the first pair.

1. **boat** is to **boats**   as   **bed** is to   <u>beds</u>

2. **penny** is to **pennies**   as   **party** is to   _____

3. **man** is to **men**   as   **woman** is to   _____

4. **dishes** is to **dish**   as   **glasses** is to   _____

5. **toy** is to **toys**   as   **key** is to   _____

6. **pennies** is to **penny**   as   **cities** is to   _____

7. **wolves** is to **wolf**   as   **knives** is to   _____

8. **key** is to **keys**   as   **birthday** is to   _____

Proofreading

B Cross out each misspelled word. Write the word correctly.

1. I onse saw some wolfes in the woods.

   _____   _____

   _____   _____

2. There is no plase to stop along this rode.

   _____   _____

   _____   _____

3. The boat docked at two citys in Maine.

_____

- - - - - - - - - -

_____

4. One of the women won the prise.

_____

- - - - - - - - -

_____

5. Get the glasas and dishs for the party.

_____   _____

- - - - - - - -   - - - - - - - -

_____   _____

6. My keys fell aut of my pocket.

_____

- - - - - -

_____

C Find the word from the box that goes in each blank.
Write each word.

knives	pennies	out	sound
coat	about	toys	boat

1. sharp _____

2. cost ten _____

3. _____ of time

4. read _____ dogs

5. row the _____

6. a winter _____

7. play with _____

8. a loud _____

A Follow these directions to complete the page.

1. Put a ✔ in front of each word that ends in **x**, **ch**, or **sh**.
   Write the plural of these words.
2. Underline each **vowel + y** word.
   Write the plural of these words.
3. Put a ⬭ around each **consonant + y** word.
   Write the plural of these words.
4. There should be four words left that have not been marked.
   Write the plural for each one.

1. brush   brushes

2. baby

3. box

4. goat

5. donkey

6. puppy

7. deer

8. bay

9. flag

10. tray

11. pony

12. lady

13. foot

14. inch

15. day

B Three words in each row follow the same spelling pattern. One word does not. Find that word. Be ready to tell why it does not belong.

1. ~~step~~   mile   lake   race

(Only the word **step** does not end with a silent **e**.)

2. south   float   toast   oak

3. feet   teeth   sheep   flies

4. count   since   around   ground

5. toads   lunches   clocks   clouds

6. cowboys   plays   candies   turkeys

7. puppy   runway   bunny   berry

C Look at the first pair of words in each row. In what way do these words go together? Write a word from the box to make the second pair of words go together in the same way as the first pair.

round   calves   candies   mouth   monkeys

1. **bones** are to **dogs**   as   **bananas** are to
(Dogs like bones.)   (Monkeys like bananas.) monkeys

2. **dog** is to **puppies**   as   **cow** is to

3. **sour** is to **lemons**   as   **sweet** is to

4. **smell** is to **nose**   as   **taste** is to

5. **box** is to **square**   as   **ball** is to

47

picnic	pile	hamburger	creek
poured	logs	lemonade	awful
grapes	ants	sparrow	bananas
burned	fire	blanket	napkins

Prewriting. Prewriting means getting ready to write. You must think about what you want to say before you begin writing.

Use Prewriting Skills

Use the spelling words to plan a story about a picnic in the woods.

1. What four things will you have to eat and drink? _____

_____ _____ _____

_____ _____ _____

2. You will need a fire to cook the food. What words go with the word **fire**?

_____ _____

_____ _____

3. What are two other things that you will bring for the picnic?

_____ _____

_____ _____

4. What three animals or other things might you see in the woods?

_____ _____ _____

_____ _____ _____

Now Think What kind of picnic will you write about? Will it be a wonderful picnic or an awful picnic? Write your story idea on your own paper.

Writing. Stories often begin with a sentence that tells the main idea or the most important thing about the story. That sentence is called a **topic sentence.**

Use Writing Skills

A On your own paper, write two good topic sentences for a story about a picnic. Begin your sentences with the word groups below.

1. Picnics can be ____.

2. On our picnic last week, ____.

A sentence must be a complete thought. Sometimes a group of words is not a sentence. You must add words to make the thought complete.

Incomplete thought: *Logs for the fire*

Complete sentence: We need more *logs for the fire.*
The *logs for the fire* are too wet to burn.

B Look at the groups of words below. Add words to make each group into a complete sentence. Write the sentences on your own paper.

1. burned the hamburgers   **4.** deer crossing the creek
2. a pile of ants   **5.** poured the lemonade
3. bananas and grapes   **6.** spilled on the blanket

Now Write   The first time you write your story is like a practice. It is called a **first draft,** or a rough draft. Write a first draft of your story. Follow the directions.

1. Begin with a topic sentence. Do you want to use one of the topic sentences you wrote for Exercise A?

2. Read the sentences you wrote for Exercise B. Will some fit your story?

Revising and Proofreading. Revising means changing parts of your story to make it better. Follow two steps to revise your writing.

1. Read your story aloud. Change any of the ideas or sentences you want to make better.
2. Proofread your writing. Look at your writing carefully to find mistakes in capitalization, punctuation, and spelling.

Use Revising and Proofreading Skills

A   Practice revising the ideas in the story below.

1. Find the two groups of words that are incomplete thoughts. Underline them.
2. On the lines below the story, make each group of words into a complete sentence by adding words.

My birthday picnic started out to be fun. Mom parked the car on a dirt road. Near the lake. First we found a good place to eat lunch. Then we put a blanket on the ground. The food, the napkins, and the dishes, too. Just as we were about to eat, we heard a loud sound. It was thunder. Suddenly, the sun was gone and one big cloud came over our picnic. Everything was soaking wet before we could count to ten. The end of my party was not much fun.

1. _____

_____

_____

2. _____

_____

B Practice your proofreading skills on the story below.

1. Cross out the six misspelled words. Write the words correctly.
2. Circle and correct two capitalization errors.
3. Circle and correct three punctuation mistakes.

Some mistakes are already marked. Mark the mistakes you find in the same way.

Remember
- A sentence begins with a capital letter and ends with a period.
- A question ends with a question mark.
- A speaker's words begin and end with quotation marks.

Sue and I went for a walk in the woods to pick berries. After a

while we found some berry bushes and began to fill our boxs.

Soon (We) heard a sound in a pile of leafs. Sue asked, "What was

that." I said, "It was just a fat old tode jumping off a stone. Then

we heard another sound. This time it was two baby bunnies   they

were chasing butterflys. we stopped onse more on the way home

to watch some sparrows. (then) we went to my house to tell

everyone about the fat old toad and the silly bunnys.

1. _____   4. _____

2. _____   5. _____

3. _____   6. _____

Now Revise   Read the first draft of your story. Be sure your sentences are complete. Proofread and correct any punctuation and spelling mistakes. Write your final copy in your best handwriting.

A Writer's Journal

UNIT TWO

You can get ideas for writing in your journal by looking at things around you. Some things—like a big red balloon or a yellow sunflower—are easy to notice. But have you ever stopped and really looked at a leaf or the bark of a tree?

Looking at things carefully can help you become a better writer. In the paragraph below, the writer tells how to look at something as simple as a leaf.

Read the paragraph. Try to picture in your mind the things the writer describes. Then discuss the questions with the class.

Look at it as though you had never seen a withered green-and-yellow leaf before in your whole life. What does it make you think of? Start with its colors. Green and yellow. Reach back into *your* private store of remembered things for pictures that match the yellow and green on the leaf. You've seen lots of yellow things, and lots of green things, and lots of yellow-and-green things. Get your notebook and write down every single one you can think of:

yellow butter and yellow butterflies and
yellow mittens and yellow beads and
yellow fish and yellow lemon drops and
yellow paper towels and a yellow sun.

Green soda bottle and green frogs and
green seesaws and green cat eyes and green giants.

Green-and-yellow tie-dyed shirts and
green-and-yellow pinwheels and
green-and-yellow turtle bellies and
green-and-yellow snakes and
green-and-yellow Play-Doh that got mixed together
by mistake.

—SYLVIA CASSEDY
from *In Your Own Words*

Talking About the Paragraph

1. What does the green-and-yellow leaf make *you* think of? What other things have *you* seen that are yellow, or green, or yellow and green?

2. What is meant by "*your* private store of remembered things"?

3. Why does the author tell you to write things in a notebook? How might the notes help you later in your other writing?

Writing in Your Journal

Maybe the paragraph has given you an idea for your next journal entry. If you need help getting started, use one of these:

1. Look around you. Choose something you see to write about. Tell what it is and what its color makes you think of.

2. Pick a color. Reach back into your memory for pictures of things that match that color. List the things you think of. For example: Orange is carrots, a jack-o-lantern, and a bright sunset.

Building a Personal Word List

When you are writing, you may want to use a word you do not know how to spell. If this happens, follow these steps:

1. Write the word as you think it should be spelled.

2. After you have finished writing, check to see if the word is on your personal word list. If not, look up the word in the dictionary.

3. Correct your spelling and add the word to your personal word list.

4. Practice spelling the word several times.

pa**ss**	*pass*
dre**ss**	*dress*
gue**ss**	*guess*
to**ss**	*toss*
acro**ss**	*across*
pre**ss**	*press*
unle**ss**	*unless*
a**ll**	*all*
pu**ll**	*pull*
fu**ll**	*full*
ro**ll**	*roll*
spe**ll**	*spell*
she**ll**	*shell*
sti**ll**	*still*
sha**ll**	*shall*

1. How many words end with the letters **ll**? _____

2. How many words end with the letters **ss**? _____

Many words end with double consonants.

54

Practice the Words

A Find pairs of spelling words that rhyme with each other and fit in the shapes. Write the words.

1.

2.

3.

4.

Proofreading

B Cross out each misspelled word. Write the word correctly.

1. Which dres shal I wear?

_____ _____

_ _ _ _ _ _ _ _ _ _ _ _ _ _ _ _ _ _ _ _ _ _

_____ _____

2. Please pass the salt accros the table.

_____

_ _ _ _ _ _ _ _ _

_____

3. I stil have all the money Dad gave me.

_____

_ _ _ _ _ _ _ _ _

_____

4. Don't pres the button unnless you want to change your answer.

_____ _____

_ _ _ _ _ _ _ _ _ _ _ _ _ _ _ _ _ _

_____ _____

Dictionary

The two words at the top of each page in the dictionary are called **guide words.** The guide word on the left tells you the first word on the page. The guide word on the right tells you the last word on the page. All the words on the page are listed in alphabetical order between the two guide words.

guide word   guide word

tall   **vest**

tall ═══════

vest ═══════

C The word pairs below are guide words. What spelling words go on each page? Write them in alphabetical order.

pass
dress
guess
toss
across
press
unless
all
pull
full
roll
spell
shell
still
shall

1. about   duck

across

2. fall   home

3. park   roof

4. shake   until

56

Writing

Write riddles for three of your spelling words. Ask a friend to guess the answers.

Use two clues in each riddle. The first clue should tell the meaning of the word. The second clue can give the number of letters, a rhyming word, or some other hint. Write your answer.

Clues

1. It means not empty.
   It sounds like pull.   full

2. _____

3. _____

4. _____

Reach Out for New Words

A Find the letters that fit in the blanks to make new words. Write each word.

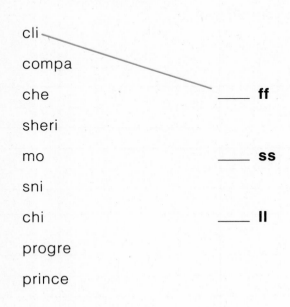

cli

compa

che   _____ **ff**

sheri

mo   _____ **ss**

sni

chi   _____ **ll**

progre

prince

1. cliff

2. _____

3. _____

4. _____

5. _____

6. _____

7. _____

8. _____

9. _____

B Use each clue to find one of the new words that fits in the boxes. You will see another new word in the colored boxes. Write each word.

1. it shows direction

2. moving ahead

3. a tall, steep mountainside

4. breathe in quickly

5. a cold feeling

6. a law officer

7. tiny green plants

8. a game like checkers

58

dollar	*dollar*
follow	*follow*
gallon	*gallon*
swallow	*swallow*
butter	*butter*
cotton	*cotton*
pretty	*pretty*
tomorrow	*tomorrow*
sorry	*sorry*
pepper	*pepper*
happen	*happen*
ribbon	*ribbon*
lesson	*lesson*
ladder	*ladder*
dinner	*dinner*

1. How many words have the letters **ll**? ____

2. How many words have the letters **tt**? ____

3. What other double letters do you see?

___ ___   ___ ___   ___ ___   ___ ___   ___ ___

Many words are spelled with double consonants in the middle.

dollar   swallow   pretty   pepper   lesson
follow   butter   tomorrow   happen   ladder
gallon   cotton   sorry   ribbon   dinner

Practice the Words

A Use each clue to find a spelling word that fits in the puzzle. Write each word.

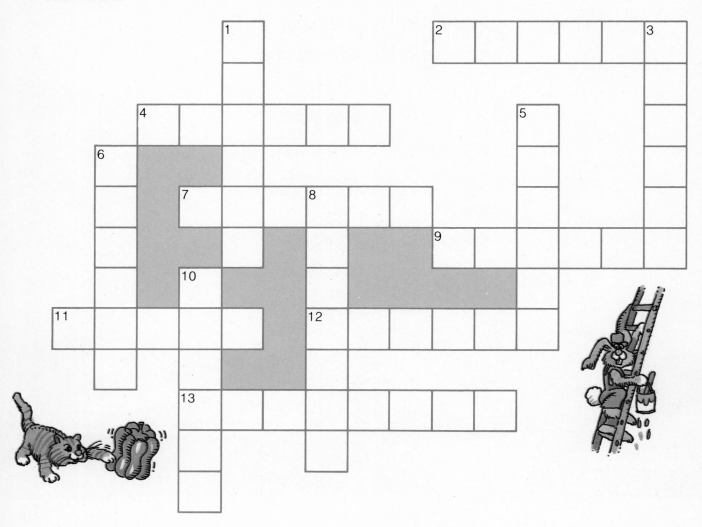

Across
2. a meal
4. used like salt
7. something to study
9. a kind of cloth
11. feeling sad
12. something to climb
13. the next day

Down
1. to take place
3. used for bows
5. spread this on bread
6. how milk is measured
8. you do this when you eat
10. beautiful

B Answer each question with spelling words.

1. Which three words have the letters **tt**?

_____   _____   _____

_____   _____   _____

2. Which four words have the letters **ll**?

_____   _____   _____

_____   _____   _____

_____

Dictionary

The words listed on a dictionary page are called **entry words**. They are printed in dark letters to help you find them.

Each entry word is divided into word parts called **syllables**. A dot or space shows where a word is divided into syllables.

but·ter (but′ ər) *noun*   a spread for bread or cooking made by churning cream.

How many syllables are in the word **butter**? _____

C Look up each word in your spelling dictionary. Divide it into syllables. Put a dot between the syllables.

1. pretty   pret·ty

2. sorry   _____

3. dinner   _____

4. dollar   _____

5. swallow   _____

6. ribbon   _____

7. happen   _____

8. ladder   _____

9. lesson   _____

10. follow   _____

11. cotton   _____

12. pepper   _____

13. gallon   _____

14. tomorrow   _____

61

Writing

Write a sentence with each group of spelling words. Circle the spelling words in each sentence. Remember to start with a capital letter and end with a period.

1. dollar, ribbon, pretty

I paid one (dollar) for this (pretty) yellow (ribbon).

2. happen, follow, ladder

3. dinner, pepper, butter

4. sorry, gallon, swallow

New Words   tennis   suddenly   million   arrow
carrot   umbrella   attic   scissors

Reach Out for New Words

A Unscramble the letters and write the new words. Look for the double consonants.

1. nistne _____

2. abmelulr _____

3. catit _____

4. rowra _____

5. csissros _____

6. nimlilo _____

7. nedysdul _____

8. arctor _____

B Complete each phrase with one of the new words.

1. not a **bow**, but an _____

2. not a **knife**, but _____

3. not **slowly**, but _____

4. not a **bean**, but a _____

5. not a **basement**, but an _____

6. not a **hundred**, but a _____

7. not **golf**, but _____

8. not a **raincoat**, but an _____

ask	+ ed =	asked	*asked*
talk	+ ed =	talked	*talked*
walk	+ ed =	walked	*walked*
shout	+ ed =	shouted	*shouted*
plant	+ ed =	planted	*planted*
close	+ ed =	closed	*closed*
live	+ ed =	lived	*lived*
use	+ ed =	used	*used*
smile	+ ed =	smiled	*smiled*
tease	+ ed =	teased	*teased*
save	+ ed =	saved	*saved*
chase	+ ed =	chased	*chased*
hike	+ ed =	hiked	*hiked*
tie	+ ed =	tied	*tied*
wade	+ ed =	waded	*waded*

A **verb** is a word that tells about an action.
A verb that tells about an action that happened in the past is
in the **past tense**.

1. The words in the first column can
   all tell about an action. They are called _____.

2. What two letters were added in the
   last column to put the verbs in the past tense? ____ ____

3. How many words in the first column end with **silent e**? ____
   What happened to the final **e** before **ed** was added? _____

Make the past tense of many verbs by adding **ed**.
When a verb ends in **silent e**, drop the **e** before you add **ed**.

A Write the spelling words that complete these sentences.

1. Alice _____ the door softly.

2. The monkeys _____ each other.

3. The painter _____ a large brush.

4. My family once _____ in Canada.

5. Tina _____ the kitten's life.

6. The teacher _____ a hard question.

7. Carl _____ to school today.

8. The dog _____ the cat up a tree.

9. The fans _____ with excitement.

10. Dad _____ on the telephone for an hour.

11. The happy child _____ at the clown.

12. We _____ a small tree in our yard.

13. Bobby _____ a bow on the present.

14. The children _____ in the shallow water.

The **base form** of a word is the word before any changes have been made.

The base form of **shouted** is **shout**.

B Read each sentence. Then follow the directions below each sentence.

1. Do you ____live____ in this building?
   (Write the base form of **lived**.)

2. Carl _____ tulips in the garden.
   (Write the past tense of **plant**.)

3. We always _____ when our team wins.
   (Write the base form of **shouted**.)

4. I _____ past that store every day.
   (Write the base form of **walked**.)

5. Ron _____ Lois to help him.
   (Write the past tense of **ask**.)

6. The farmer will _____ a strong hoe.
   (Write the base form of **used**.)

7. The owners _____ the store at night.
   (Write the base form of **closed**.)

8. My sister _____ her money.
   (Write the past tense of **save**.)

9. The scouts _____ through the forest.
   (Write the past tense of **hike**.)

10. Do all dogs _____ cars?
    (Write the base form of **chased**.)

asked	shouted	lived	teased	hiked
talked	planted	used	saved	tied
walked	closed	smiled	chased	waded

C Unscramble each group of letters to make a word. Write each word. Then add **ed** to each word to make it a spelling word.

1. klaw _____ _____

2. touhs _____ _____

3. vile _____ _____

4. secol _____ _____

5. kalt _____ _____

6. seate _____ _____

7. miles _____ _____

8. keih _____ _____

9. iet _____ _____

10. dewa _____ _____

Build Word Power

Each word below is part of a spelling word. Write the spelling word.

1. mile   smiled   5. ease _____

2. us _____   6. has _____

3. ant _____   7. out _____

4. lose _____   8. as _____

Search for new words!

Follow the directions below.

Reach Out for New Words

A In this puzzle, each number is written twice. Find the silent **e** word in each pair of numbers. Connect the numbered dots that go with the **silent e** words.

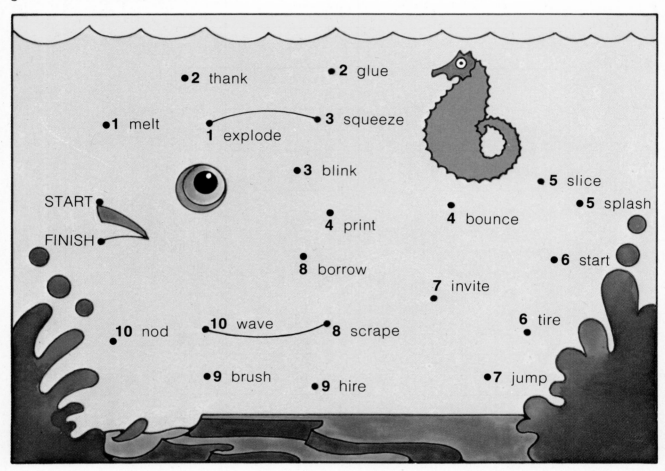

●2 thank   ●2 glue

●1 melt   1 explode   ●3 squeeze

●3 blink

START●   ●5 slice

●4 print   ●5 splash

FINISH●   4 bounce

8 borrow   ●6 start

7 invite

10 nod   10 wave   8 scrape   6 tire

●9 brush   ●7 jump

●9 hire

B Write the past tense of each new **silent e** word.

1. _____   6. _____

2. _____   7. _____

3. _____   8. _____

4. _____   9. _____

5. _____   10. _____

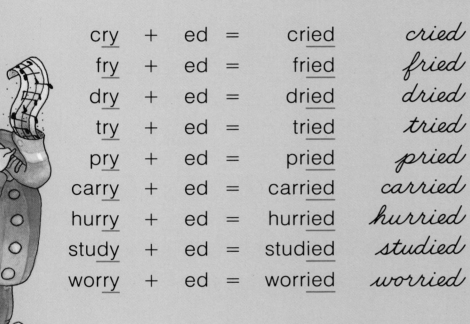

play	+ ed =	played	*played*
stay	+ ed =	stayed	*stayed*
spray	+ ed =	sprayed	*sprayed*
sway	+ ed =	swayed	*swayed*
obey	+ ed =	obeyed	*obeyed*
enjoy	+ ed =	enjoyed	*enjoyed*
cry	+ ed =	cried	*cried*
fry	+ ed =	fried	*fried*
dry	+ ed =	dried	*dried*
try	+ ed =	tried	*tried*
pry	+ ed =	pried	*pried*
carry	+ ed =	carried	*carried*
hurry	+ ed =	hurried	*hurried*
study	+ ed =	studied	*studied*
worry	+ ed =	worried	*worried*

1. The words in the first column can all be action words or _____.

2. How many words in the first column end with **vowel + y**? ____
   Is the base word changed before **ed** is added? _____

3. How many verbs in the first column end with **consonant + y**? ____
   Change the ____ to ____ before you add **ed**.

4. The verbs in the last column are in the _____ tense.

When a verb ends with **vowel + y**, add the ending **ed** to make the past tense.
When a verb ends with **consonant + y**, change the **y** to **i** before you add **ed**.

played	swayed	cried	tried	hurried
stayed	obeyed	fried	pried	studied
sprayed	enjoyed	dried	carried	worried

Practice the Words

A Write the spelling words that complete these sentences.

1. The sun _____ up the puddles.

2. Linda was late so she _____ to school.

3. I _____ eating the _____ chicken.

4. The children _____ indoors and _____ games.

5. The pirates _____ open the treasure chest.

6. We _____ the bags to the car.

7. My baby brother _____ all night.

8. Jane _____ not to laugh.

9. Tom _____ for the math test.

10. The trees _____ back and forth in the wind.

70

B Add the missing letters to complete these spelling words. Then write the base words.

1. c __ i __ d _____

2. o __ e __ e __ _____

3. s __ r __ y __ d _____

4. w __ r __ i __ d _____

C Write the past tense of each base word that fits in the puzzle.

Across	**Down**
2. stay	**1.** carry
4. hurry	**2.** study
6. spray	**3.** play
8. worry	**5.** enjoy
11. fry	**7.** sway
12. dry	**9.** pry
13. obey	**10.** try

played	swayed	cried	tried	hurried
stayed	obeyed	fried	pried	studied
sprayed	enjoyed	dried	carried	worried

Build Word Power

Writing

Make up an answer for each question. Use the past tense of the underlined word when you write your sentence.

1. What games did the children <u>play</u>?

_____

- -

_____

- -

_____

2. What did your class <u>study</u> this morning?

_____

- -

_____

- -

_____

3. How many of those boxes did you <u>carry</u> upstairs?

_____

- -

_____

- -

_____

4. Where did Luis <u>stay</u> when his parents were away?

_____

- -

_____

- -

_____

5. What did you <u>enjoy</u> most about the circus?

_____

- -

_____

- -

_____

New Words   decay   spy   multiply   destroy   marry
reply   delay   employ   bury   deny

Reach Out for New Words

A Write each new word in the correct column.

vowel + y words   **consonant + y words**

Dictionary

B Look up each word in your spelling dictionary. Divide it into
syllables. Put a dot between the syllables. Then write the past
tense.

1. reply   re·ply   replied

2. marry

3. delay

4. destroy

5. spy

6. multiply

7. deny

8. decay

9. bury

10. employ

Irregular past tense

lay	laid	*lay*	*laid*
say	said	*say*	*said*
see	saw	*see*	*saw*
fly	flew	*fly*	*flew*
take	took	*take*	*took*
write	wrote	*write*	*wrote*
wake	woke	*wake*	*woke*
win	won	*win*	*won*
ride	rode	*ride*	*rode*
fall	fell	*fall*	*fell*
hold	held	*hold*	*held*
swim	swam	*swim*	*swam*
send	sent	*send*	*sent*
build	built	*build*	*built*
go	went	*go*	*went*

1. The words in the first column can all be action words or _____.

2. The verbs in the second column are in the _____ tense.

3. Do the verbs in the second column have the ending **ed**? _____

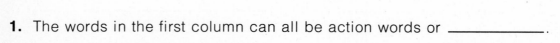

Some verbs do not add the ending **ed** to make the past tense.
A new word is used.

Practice the Words

A Write these words in alphabetical order in the first column. Then complete the chart.

wake   see   say   go   fall

write   win   build   fly   swim

hold   lay   ride   take   send

Word	Past Tense	How many letters are the same?
build	built	4

A **synonym** is a word that means almost the same as another word.
An **antonym** is a word that means the opposite of another word.

B Complete each sentence with a spelling word.

1. A synonym for **looked** is _____.

2. An antonym for **lost** is _____.

3. An antonym for **slept** is _____.

4. A synonym for **tripped** is _____.

5. An antonym for **gave** is _____.

6. A synonym for **talked** is _____.

7. A synonym for **left** is _____.

8. An antonym for **dropped** is _____.

Proofreading

C Cross out each misspelled word. Write the word correctly.

1. The robin flue to its nest and layed an egg.

_____   _____

2. Last summer I suam and road my bike.

_____   _____

3. Bob cent me a story he rote.

_____   _____

4. Val fell out of the tree house she biult.

_____

laid	flew	woke	fell	sent
said	took	won	held	built
saw	wrote	rode	swam	went

Build Word Power

Writing

Write a sentence to answer each question. Use the past tense of
the underlined word in your sentence.

1. What time did you <u>wake</u> up this morning?

_____

_____

2. What did you <u>write</u> your story about?

_____

_____

3. Which animals did you <u>see</u> at the zoo?

_____

_____

4. Where did you <u>ride</u> your bike?

_____

_____

5. Where did you <u>go</u> this summer?

_____

_____

Reach Out for New Words

A The new words are the past tense forms of the verbs below. Find
each new word and circle it. Write each word you find next to the
correct verb. The words are printed in three directions in the
puzzle. → ↓ ↘

u	x	w	h	g	b	f	z	g	f
q	n	v	s	t	m	d	d	g	c
f	e	d	p	b	j	u	p	k	p
x	w	z	e	m	q	g	n	h	l
k	l	v	n	r	b	f	x	z	d
h	c	i	t	s	s	s	j	b	a
w	w	s	w	e	p	t	d	m	c
r	p	q	s	o	v	o	o	n	l
y	f	d	t	r	r	l	t	o	s
o	k	n	t	o	r	e	j	r	d

1. feed _____

2. sweep _____

3. tear _____

4. wear _____

5. spend _____

6. dig _____

7. steal _____

8. understand _____

B Write the past tense of each verb. Then tell how you changed the
verb to its past tense.

1. wear _____wore_____ Change __ear__ to __ore__

2. steal _____ Change _____ to _____

3. dig _____ Change _____ to _____

4. tear _____ Change _____ to _____

5. feed _____ Drop one _____ _____

6. sweep _____ Change _____ to _____

7. spend _____ Change _____ to _____

8. understand _____ Change _____ to _____

keep + ing = keeping *keeping*
find + ing = finding *finding*
clean + ing = cleaning *cleaning*
spend + ing = spending *spending*
buy + ing = buying *buying*
say + ing = saying *saying*
hurry + ing = hurrying *hurrying*

trace + ing = tracing *tracing*
freeze + ing = freezing *freezing*
bore + ing = boring *boring*
drive + ing = driving *driving*
move + ing = moving *moving*
rise + ing = rising *rising*
have + ing = having *having*
come + ing = coming *coming*

1. What ending was added to the verbs in the first column to make the verbs in the last column? _____

2. How many verbs in the first column end with **silent e**? ____

3. Look at the **silent e** words. What letter was dropped before **ing** was added? ____

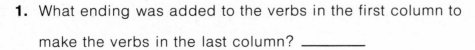

The ending **ing** can be added to many words.
When a verb ends with **silent e**, drop the **e** before you add **ing**.

Practice the Words

A Write the spelling words that complete these sentences.

1. Ted is _____ his messy room.

2. Mom likes _____ our new car.

3. Allen slept through the _____ movie.

4. Mario is _____ popcorn for the movie.

5. The sun is _____ in the east.

6. Jane is _____ the outline of the map.

7. Kim has been _____ her money on candy.

8. JoAnne is _____ to the game with us.

9. The firefighters were _____ to the fire.

10. Lyle's family is _____ to another town.

11. My toes are _____ from the cold.

12. The hen is _____ her eggs warm.

13. Can you hear what Mrs. Wilson is _____ ?

80

keeping	spending	hurrying	boring	rising
finding	buying	tracing	driving	having
cleaning	saying	freezing	moving	coming

B Find the misspelled word in each group. Write the word correctly.

1. haveing

writing

buying

carrying

_____

- - - - - - - - -

_____

2. liking

keeping

fineding

dancing

_____

- - - - - - - - -

_____

3. driving

spending

moving

traceing

_____

- - - - - - - - -

_____

Dictionary

Each dictionary entry is made up of an entry word and all the information that follows it.

Many entry words are base words. Words with endings, or **word forms**, are often included in the base word entry.

find (fīnd) *verb* to get back something that has been lost [We *found* the missing book.]
—**found, find′ ing**

For example, the word form **finding** is included in the entry for **find**.

C Write the entry word you would look up to find each word.

_____

- - - - - - - -

1. finding _____

- - - - - - - -

2. buying _____

- - - - - - - -

3. driving _____

- - - - - - - -

4. moving _____

- - - - - - - -

5. keeping _____

- - - - - - - -

6. saying _____

- - - - - - - -

7. rising _____

_____

- - - - - - - -

8. cleaning _____

- - - - - - - -

9. spending _____

- - - - - - - -

10. hurrying _____

- - - - - - - -

11. having _____

- - - - - - - -

12. freezing _____

- - - - - - - -

13. boring _____

- - - - - - - -

14. coming _____

keeping	spending	hurrying	boring	rising
finding	buying	tracing	driving	having
cleaning	saying	freezing	moving	coming

Build Word Power

Find the spelling word that means the opposite of each word or phrase. Write the word. Then write its base form.

	Spelling Word	**Base Form**
1. going	coming	come
2. making a mess		
3. moving slowly		
4. giving away		
5. saving		
6. losing		
7. boiling		
8. standing still		
9. interesting		
10. sinking		

New Words   argue   share   change   watch
              bother   praise   leave   scurry

Reach Out for New Words

A Unscramble each group of letters to make the **ing** form of one of the new words. Write the **ing** words.

1. grashin _____

2. chigntwa _____

3. nasipirg _____

4. gleaniv _____

5. ragginu _____

6. higgannc _____

7. snurgircy _____

8. notrbhige _____

B Write the **ing** form of each new word that matches each meaning.

1. saying good things _____

2. going away _____

3. looking at _____

4. making different _____

5. giving some to others _____

6. running quickly _____

7. quarreling _____

8. pestering _____

pin	pinned	pinning	*pinned*	*pinning*
wag	wagged	wagging	*wagged*	*wagging*
beg	begged	begging	*begged*	*begging*
stop	stopped	stopping	*stopped*	*stopping*
skip	skipped	skipping	*skipped*	*skipping*
plan	planned	planning	*planned*	*planning*
tag	tagged	tagging	*tagged*	*tagging*
tip	tipped	tipping	*tipped*	*tipping*

1. Look at the words in the first column.

   How many syllables does each word have? ____

   How many vowels does each word have? ____

   How many consonants are at the end of each word? ____

2. When the endings **ed** and **ing** are added to each word, what

   happens to the final consonant? _____

Words that have **1 syllable**   pin
                and **1 vowel**   pin
   and end with **1 consonant**   pin
      follow what is called the **1 + 1 + 1 spelling pattern**.
   Double the final consonant before you add **ed** or **ing**.

A Print the spelling word that fits in the shapes and rhymes with the clue word.

1. dragging

w a g g i n g

2. ripping

3. dripped

4. winning

5. bragged

6. mopped

7. pegged

8. fanned

9. hopping

10. sagged

11. grinned

12. fanning

pinned	pinning	skipped	skipping
wagged	wagging	planned	planning
begged	begging	tagged	tagging
stopped	stopping	tipped	tipping

B Unscramble each group of letters to make the base form of a spelling word. Write the base form. Then write the **ing** form.

1. kips _____ _____

2. geb _____ _____

3. nalp _____ _____

4. agt _____ _____

5. pots _____ _____

6. nip _____ _____

7. awg _____ _____

8. itp _____ _____

Dictionary

C Write the dictionary entry word you would look up to find each word below.

1. pinned _____   5. begging _____

2. tagging _____   6. planned _____

3. tipped _____   7. wagged _____

4. skipped _____   8. stopped _____

Writing

Sometimes two sentences tell about ideas that are alike. The sentences may even use some of the same words.

Debbie is planning a party. <u>She is planning a party</u> for Val.

You can put these two sentences together to make one sentence. The underlined words in the second sentence are not needed in the new sentence.

Debbie is planning a party for Val.

Make one sentence from each pair of sentences. The words you do not need in the new sentence are underlined.

1. The bus stopped. <u>It stopped</u> at the corner.

2. Sue is skipping rope. <u>She is skipping</u> as fast as she can.

3. The dog is wagging his tail. <u>He is wagging it</u> because he is happy.

Search for new words!
Follow the directions below.

Reach Out for New Words

A Find the right path through this maze. The words on the correct path follow the **1 + 1 + 1 pattern**. Write the **ed** form of each word.

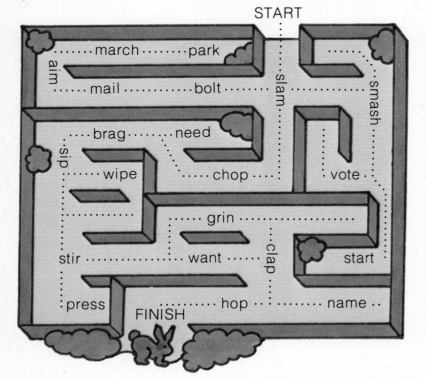

START

march ······ park

aim

mail ······ bolt ······ slam ······ smash

brag ····· need

sip

wipe ····· chop ····· vote

grin

stir ····· want ····· clap ····· start

press

hop ····· name

FINISH

1. _____

2. _____

3. _____

4. _____

5. _____

6. _____

7. _____

8. _____

B Use each clue to think of the **ing** form of a word you found in the maze. Each word should fit in the puzzle. Write the words. Then read the new **ing** word you see in the colored boxes.

1. closing loudly

2. jumping

3. cutting

4. hitting hands

5. drinking

6. mixing

7. smiling

8. boasting

88

10.
guess
dress
spell

11.
dollar
sorry
pretty

12.
talk   talked
walk   walked
save   saved

13.
play   played
try   tried
study   studied

14.
say   said
ride   rode
fall   fell

15.
buy   buying
hurry   hurrying
move   moving

16.
tip   tipped   tipping
stop   stopped   stopping
plan   planned   planning

A Look at the first pair of words in each row. In what way do these words go together? Write a spelling word that makes the second pair of words go together in the same way as the first pair.

1. **study** is to **studied**   as   **try** is to   _____

2. **play** is to **playing**   as   **buy** is to   _____

3. **plan** is to **planning**   as   **stop** is to   _____

4. **study** is to **studying**   as   **hurry** is to   _____

5. **say** is to **said**   as   **ride** is to   _____

6. **rode** is to **ride**   as   **fell** is to   _____

7. **save** is to **saving**   as   **move** is to   _____

8. **dropped** is to **drop**   as   **tipped** is to   _____

Proofreading

B Cross out each misspelled word. Write the word correctly.

1. I tiped over the prety vase of flowers.

_____   _____

_____   _____

2. Larry tried to spel the long word.

_____

_____

3. Ann siad, "I'm planing on wearing this dress."

_____   _____

_____   _____

4. We wawked to the park and plaied baseball.

_____   _____

_____   _____

C Write the word from the box that goes in each blank.

studied	saved	talked	dollar
dress	guess	sorry	fell

1. I _____ on the phone.

2. I _____ my money.

3. We _____ for the test.

4. I'll _____ the answer.

5. He _____ on the ice.

6. I'm very _____ .

7. She wore a _____ .

8. He spent a _____ .

Using More Review Words

A Follow these directions.

1. Put a ☐ around each **silent e** word. Write the past tense.

2. Underline each **vowel + y** word. Write the past tense.

3. Put a ⬭ around each **consonant + y** word. Write the past tense.

4. Put a * after each **1 + 1 + 1 word**. Write the past tense.

5. Write the past tense of the three words you have left.

1. │close│   closed

2. spray

3. clean

4. plant

5. stay

6. ask

7. obey

8. tip

9. smile

10. study

11. use

12. pry

13. skip

14. tag

15. carry

92

B Three words in each row follow the same spelling pattern. One word does not. Find that word. Be ready to tell why it does not belong.

1. across   pass   pull   ~~gallon~~
   (Only **gallon** has the double letter in the middle.)

2. boring   keeping   freezing   driving

3. woke   rode   pinned   wrote

4. obeyed   worried   dried   fried

5. wagging   spending   begging   tipping

6. trace   rise   have   unless

7. closed   asked   teased   lived

C Look at the first pair of words in each row. Then write a word from the box that makes the second pair of words go together in the same way as the first pair.

dinner   shouted   off   full   tomorrow   flew

1. **in** is to **out**   as   **on** is to   _____

2. **present** is to **future**   as   **today** is to   _____

3. **fish** is to **swam**   as   **bird** is to   _____

4. **bottom** is to **top**   as   **empty** is to   _____

5. **noon** is to **lunch**   as   **evening** is to   _____

6. **quiet** is to **whispered**   as   **loud** is to   _____

SPELLING AND THE PROCESS OF WRITING

milk	sting	pail	rooster
pint	stung	wagon	pumpkin
bees	dozen	honey	turnips
colt	hogs	basket	cabbage

Prewriting. Prewriting means getting ready to write. You must think about what you want to say before you begin writing.

Use Prewriting Skills

Use the spelling words to plan a story about a farm.

1. What four animals might be on the farm? _____

_____   _____   _____

2. What five foods are on the farm? _____ _____

_____   _____   _____

3. What three things can you use for carrying?

_____   _____   _____

4. What two words go with **bee**?

_____   _____

Now Think Think about what a person might see and do on a farm. Do you want to tell a story about someone who visits a farm or someone who lives there? What will the farm look like? Write your story ideas on your own paper.

Writing. A story tells about something that happens. It has a beginning, a middle, and an ending. Where a story happens is called the **setting**.

Use Writing Skills

A Copy each topic sentence below. Choose one word from each pair. See how the words change the setting.

1. Mr. Kapp's (dairy, cattle) farm is a (busy, lonely) place to (live, visit) in the middle of (summer, winter).

2. The morning (frost, sunshine) felt (warm, chilly) as we (walked, ran) to the (barn, field) to help Aunt Laura.

Several ideas can be put together in one sentence. Use commas to separate items in a series of three or more things.

When I woke up, I heard a
   rooster crowing.
I heard bees buzzing.
I heard dogs barking.

When I woke up, I heard a
rooster crowing, bees
buzzing, and dogs barking.

B On your paper, practice putting ideas together into one sentence.

1. Sue was carrying a pail of milk.
   She was carrying a dozen eggs.
   She was carrying a jar of honey.

   Sue was carrying ____ .

2. We saw two fat hogs in the barnyard.
   We saw a skinny colt.
   We saw a red rooster.

   In the barnyard, we saw ____ .

Now Write Write the first draft of your farm story. Follow these directions.

1. Begin with a topic sentence that tells about the setting.
2. Decide what will happen in your story. How will it begin? How will it end?

Revising. Revising means changing parts of your story to make it better. Follow two steps to revise your writing.

1. Read your story aloud. Change or add anything that would make it sound better.
2. Proofread your story. Look at your writing carefully to find mistakes in capitalization, punctuation, and spelling.

Use Revising and Proofreading Skills

A Revise the ideas in the story below. Mark the changes. Then copy the revised story on your own paper.

1. Find a place where a word is missing. Mark the place with a **carat** (∧) and add the missing word.
2. Find an incomplete thought. Add words to make a complete sentence.
3. Underline three sentences that would sound better if they were written as one sentence. As you rewrite, remember to add commas.
4. Draw two lines under the sentence that would be a good beginning sentence. It tells about the setting. When you rewrite the story, put this sentence first.

I tripped over a pail of milk and scared Kevin. He jumped and dropped the basket of eggs. The inside of the old barn looked spooky when the door closed behind us. We stood still and listened. Squeaking noises. We started looking around. The noises were coming the hay wagon.

"Look!" I said. "It's a cat who came in to have her babies."

The mother cat meowed. Six new kittens were lying beside her. She had two black kittens. She had two white kittens. She had two spotted kittens. Kevin laughed and said, "I never knew cats could squeak like mice!"

B Practice your proofreading skills on the story below.

1. Cross out the six misspelled words. Write them correctly.
2. Circle and correct four capitalization errors.
3. Circle and correct three punctuation mistakes.

Some mistakes are already marked. Mark the mistakes you find in the same way.

Remember
- A sentence begins with a capital letter and ends with a period.
- Common nouns are not capitalized.
- A comma separates a series of three or more things.

Our Class visit to the animal farm was fun. We were

able to pet and feed the animals. The (Farm) had dozins

of fences but no cages. Inside the first fence, we petted

two coults We fed them some oats from a pale Then we fed the

sheep the hogs and the Goats. One silly goat tried to eat my

lunch baskit and my pumkin pie. Finally, we went to the best

place of all. it was a dirt track for pony rides. After we rode on

the ponies, a few of us rode around the track in a wagen pulled

by a Donkey.

1. _____   4. _____

2. _____   5. _____

3. _____   6. _____

Now Revise   Read the first draft of your story. Be sure your sentences are complete. Check that your story has a beginning, a middle, and an end. Proofread and correct mistakes in capitalization, punctuation, and spelling. Write your final copy in your best handwriting.

A Writer's Journal

UNIT THREE

Ideas for writing in your journal can come from reading. In the poem below, the writer talks about certain smells. How can something written on a piece of paper help you remember how things smell?

Read this poem. See if the words and phrases the writer uses help you remember smells. Then discuss the questions with your class.

> **"THINK OF TREE"**
>
> Under
> the car smell
>
> over
> the tar smell
>
> a sweet green and far smell
> flows
> down the street.
>
> And it says
> drifting by,
>   "Think of tree.
>   Think of sky.
>   Think of ripe apples
>   and hay, sun-dry."
>
> Then you know—
> not far away
> they are cutting grass
> in the park today.
>
> —LILIAN MOORE

Talking About the Poem

1. Where does the speaker in the poem live? How can you tell?
2. Where might the speaker have smelled trees and ripe apples? Where might he or she have smelled sun-dried hay?
3. What is the "sweet green and far smell"?
4. What are some of your favorite outdoor smells?

Now read this paragraph. It is from the book *In Your Own Words* by Sylvia Cassedy. It talks about how to sharpen your sense of smell.

Talking About the Paragraph

1. You often hear quiet sounds, but what are quiet smells?
2. What are some ways of discovering quiet smells?

Writing in Your Journal

The poem and the paragraph may have given you ideas about things that may have quiet smells and how you can write about them. Here are some ideas you might use if you need them.

1. Choose your favorite smell—something like bread baking, an orange being peeled, popcorn popping, or the air outside after it rains. Write one sentence about that smell so that someone else could smell it.
2. What is a quiet smell you discovered "by accident"? Describe the smell and how you discovered it.

Some objects that surround you all the time have little quiet smells that you hardly know about. Find out what some of them are. Walk around your living room some time when you don't have a cold, and press your nose against a sofa cushion, a wooden table, the back of the television, a lampshade, a shiny magazine, a telephone book, the soil in a flowerpot. Sometimes you discover these smells by accident, when you are crying into a pillow, for instance, or resting your head on your homework notebook.

Building a Personal Word List

Keeping a personal word list can help you become a better speller. First, the list shows you the words you need to learn to spell. Second, it can help you figure out the kinds of spelling mistakes you make.

As you add words to your personal word list, notice the kinds of spelling mistakes you made. Maybe you forgot to change the **y** to **i** when you wrote **fried**. If you know what kinds of spelling mistakes you make, you may be able to keep them from happening.

fork	*fork*
born	*born*
corn	*corn*
horn	*horn*
north	*north*
sport	*sport*
shorts	*shorts*
storm	*storm*
story	*story*
forget	*forget*
word	*word*
worm	*worm*
world	*world*
worth	*worth*
worst	*worst*

1. What two letters do you see in every word? ____ ____

2. In how many words do the letters **or** sound like the word **or**? ____

3. In how many words do the letters **or** sound like **er** in the word **her**? ____

Many words are spelled with the letters **or**.
The letters **or** may have different sounds.

Practice the Words

A Write the spelling words that complete these sentences.

1. Val likes to eat _____ on the cob.

2. I use a _____ to eat my french fries.

3. Soccer is Nancy's favorite _____ .

4. Bob read a _____ about a giant.

5. The _____ kept us awake all night.

6. Lee saw a _____ crawling in the dirt.

7. My baby brother was _____ in January.

8. I spelled one _____ wrong on the test.

9. Canada is _____ of the United States.

10. A globe is a round map of the _____ .

11. I like to wear _____ in hot weather.

12. My sister plays a _____ in the band.

13. Did you _____ your lunch money again?

14. How much is that diamond ring _____ ?

fork	horn	shorts	forget	world
born	north	storm	word	worth
corn	sport	story	worm	worst

B Look at each word. If it is spelled correctly, draw a 😊. If it is misspelled, write the word correctly.

1. *story* _____

2. *werm* _____

3. *spowrt* _____

4. *world* _____

5. *werth* _____

6. *forek* _____

7. *born* _____

8. *noreth* _____

9. *werd* _____

10. *wurst* _____

11. *horn* _____

12. *fourget* _____

C Use each clue to find a spelling word that fits in the puzzle. Write each word.

1. opposite of **best**

2. a trumpet

3. a yellow vegetable

4. the earth

5. a fairy tale

6. thunder and lightning

Write the word that you see in the colored boxes. _____

102

Writing

A **cinquain** is a poem that has five lines.

Line **1**: a noun

Line **2**: two words <u>describing</u> the noun

Line **3**: three words telling <u>actions</u> of the noun

Line **4**: four words giving a <u>thought</u> or <u>feeling</u> about the noun

Line **5**: a word that means the same as the noun

Storm

Wild, windy

Blows, shrieks, howls

Makes me feel afraid

Tornado

Write cinquains using two of your spelling words.

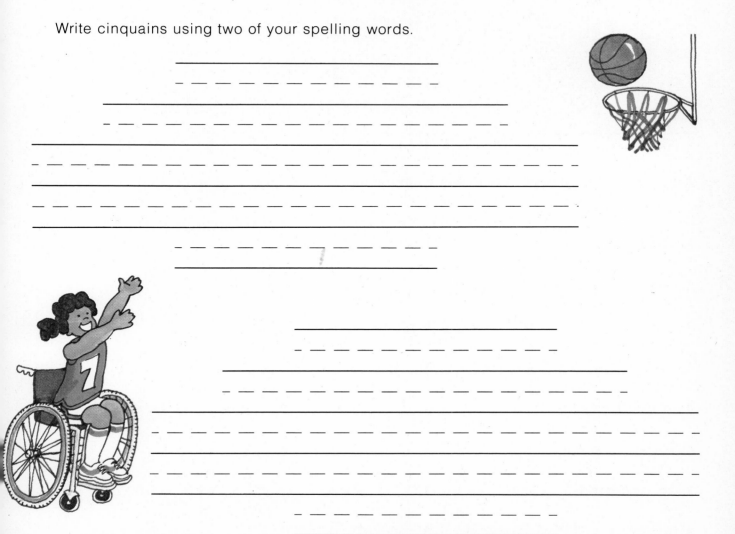

Reach Out for New Words

A Find the eight new **or** words in this puzzle. Circle each word and write it. Some of the words may overlap.

1. _____

2. _____

3. _____

4. _____

5. _____

6. _____

7. _____

8. _____

B Write the new **or** word that matches each meaning.

1. a port   1. _____

2. a sharp needle on a plant   2. _____

3. a nut   3. _____

4. where two streets cross   4. _____

5. a wind storm   5. _____

6. it plays music   6. _____

7. to command   7. _____

8. forward   8. _____

paper	*paper*
never	*never*
river	*river*
later	*later*
under	*under*
winter	*winter*
summer	*summer*
number	*number*
over	*over*
water	*water*
herd	*herd*
person	*person*
very	*very*
every	*every*
America	*America*

What two letters do you see in every word? ____ ____

Many words are spelled with the letters **er**.

paper   later   summer   water   very

never   under   number   herd   every

river   winter   over   person   America

Practice the Words

A Use each clue to find a spelling word that fits in the puzzle. Write each word.

Across

6. 8 is a _____

7. a human being

9. each

10. a large stream

13. a cold season

14. not sooner

Down

1. opposite of **under**

2. a hot season

3. what you write on

4. below

5. Today is _____ hot.

8. not ever

11. what's in a lake

12. group of cows

Proofreading

B Cross out the misspelled word in each phrase below. Write the
word correctly.

1. *number your paeper* _____

2. *hered of elephants* _____

3. *have nevre seen* _____

4. *verry cold winter* _____

5. *evrey person in the room* _____

6. *later this sumer* _____

7. *very deep rivir* _____

8. *undr the bridge* _____

9. *United States of Amaerica* _____

10. *a glass of watter* _____

Dictionary

C All of these words are entry words in a dictionary. Look up each word
and show how it is divided. Put a dot between the syllables.

_____

1. winter _____

2. over _____

3. later _____

4. number _____

5. paper _____

6. never _____

7. person _____

8. America _____

paper	later	summer	water	very
never	under	number	herd	every
river	winter	over	person	America

Build Word Power

Writing

Write four silly sentences. Use two or more **er** words in each sentence. Circle those words.

1. _The (river) freezes every (summer)._

2. _____

3. _____

4. _____

5. _____

Search for new words!
Follow the directions below.

Reach Out for New Words

A Look at the word in each space. Color the space red if the word
has the letters **er**. Color the other spaces blue. Write the words
from the red spaces.

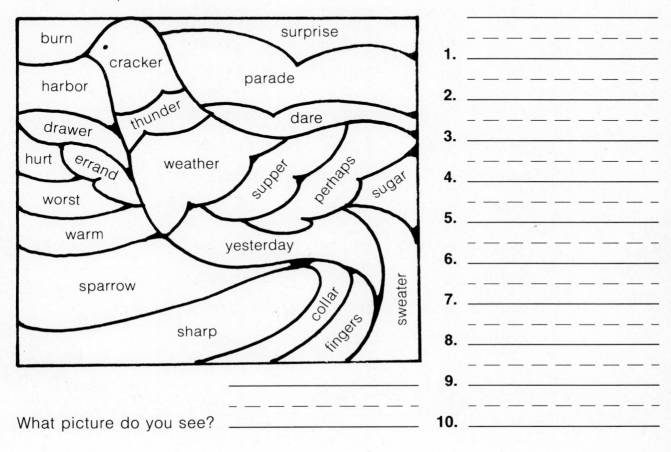

burn
surprise
cracker
harbor
parade
thunder
drawer
dare
hurt   errand   weather   supper   perhaps   sugar
worst
warm   yesterday
sparrow
collar
fingers
sweater
sharp

1. _____

2. _____

3. _____

4. _____

5. _____

6. _____

7. _____

8. _____

9. _____

10. _____

What picture do you see? _____

B Unscramble each group of letters to make one of the words you
found in the puzzle.

1. styaydeer _____

2. draner _____

3. darrew _____

4. happers _____

5. reathew _____

6. kaccerr _____

7. treeaws _____

8. trudneh _____

9. sreppu _____

10. ringsef _____

Nouns formed with er

work + er =	worker	*worker*	
lead + er =	leader	*leader*	
paint + er =	painter	*painter*	
pitch + er =	pitcher	*pitcher*	
copy + er =	copier	*copier*	
fly + er =	flier	*flier*	
carry + er =	carrier	*carrier*	
dancé + er =	dancer	*dancer*	
baké + er =	baker	*baker*	
skaté + er =	skater	*skater*	
wipé + er =	wiper	*wiper*	
win + er =	winner	*winner*	
shop + er =	shopper	*shopper*	
swim + er =	swimmer	*swimmer*	
zip + er =	zipper	*zipper*	

1. The words in the first column are verbs. What two letters have been added to all of the words in the last column? ____ ____

2. How many verbs in the first column end with **consonant + y**? ____

   Change the ____ to ____ before you add **er**.

3. How many verbs end with **silent e**? ____ Drop the ____ before you add **er**.

4. How many verbs follow the **1 + 1 + 1 spelling pattern**? ____

   Double the final _____ before you add **er**.

When **er** is added to a verb, the new word tells who or what is doing the action.

110

A Write the spelling words that complete these sentences.

1. The _____ made rolls and cakes.

2. The sales clerk helped the _____ .

3. Our car needs one new windshield _____ .

4. The _____ fell on the ice.

5. The band _____ raised his arms.

6. The _____ on my jacket is broken.

7. The _____ jumped into the pool.

8. The _____ put on her tap shoes.

9. Tom was the _____ of the race.

10. The airline pilot enjoys being a _____ .

11. The _____ is cleaning her brushes.

12. That beaver is a hard _____ .

13. The _____ struck out three batters in a row.

14. A mail _____ brings the mail to our house.

B Write the spelling word that matches each meaning.

1. someone who flies _____

2. someone who skates _____

3. someone who dances _____

4. someone who leads _____

5. someone who bakes _____

6. someone who wins _____

7. someone who paints _____

8. someone who swims _____

9. something that zips _____

10. something that makes copies _____

C Find the misspelled word in each group. Write the word correctly.

1. baker
   worker
   carier
   dancer

   _____

2. flier
   leader
   swimmer
   wipper

   _____

3. picher
   shopper
   painter
   baker

   _____

4. zipper
   shoper
   dancer
   leader

   _____

5. werker
   skater
   winner
   flier

   _____

6. painter
   shopper
   copyer
   swimmer

   _____

worker	pitcher	carrier	skater	shopper
leader	copier	dancer	wiper	swimmer
painter	flier	baker	winner	zipper

Build Word Power

Follow the **+** and **−** signs to change each clue word into a spelling word.

1. pointer   −o   +a   = _____

2. danger   −g   +c   = _____

3. shipper   −i   +o   = _____

4. shaker   −sh   +b   = _____

5. spinner   −sp   +w   = _____

6. walker   −al   +or   = _____

7. floor   −oo   +ie   = _____

8. glimmer   −gl   +sw   = _____

9. catcher   −ca   +pi   = _____

10. louder   −ou   +ea   = _____

Reach Out for New Words

A Write each new word in the correct column.

consonant + y	silent e	1 + 1 + 1 word	others
_____	_____	_____	_____
_____	_____	_____	_____
	_____	_____	_____
		_____	
		_____	

B Words are printed in three different directions in this puzzle. → ↓ ↘
Find the **er** forms of the nine new words. Circle the words in the
puzzle. Then write each word.

```
d  i  p  p  e  r  b  b  d  q
r  t  v  d  y  s  x  w  z  c
u  f  r  c  r  l  k  s  p  a
m  j  s  d  q  o  b  u  f  t
m  n  t  p  r  z  p  p  q  c
e  r  a  s  e  r  x  p  w  h
r  w  p  m  p  a  p  l  e  e
g  k  l  h  c  h  k  i  v  r
h  s  e  g  r  j  m  e  t  n
k  j  r  l  m  g  f  r  r  d
s  p  i  n  n  e  r  l  c  n
```

1. _____
2. _____
3. _____
4. _____
5. _____
6. _____
7. _____
8. _____
9. _____

wind + y = windy   *windy*
sand + y = sandy   *sandy*
salt + y = salty   *salty*
luck + y = lucky   *lucky*
sleep + y = sleepy   *sleepy*

icé + y = icy   *icy*
smoké + y = smoky   *smoky*
shadé + y = shady   *shady*
shiné + y = shiny   *shiny*
grimé + y = grimy   *grimy*

su<u>n</u> + y = su<u>nn</u>y   *sunny*
fo<u>g</u> + y = fo<u>gg</u>y   *foggy*
fu<u>n</u> + y = fu<u>nn</u>y   *funny*
mu<u>d</u> + y = mu<u>dd</u>y   *muddy*
ba<u>g</u> + y = ba<u>gg</u>y   *baggy*

An **adjective** is a word that describes something.

1. What letter was added to all of the nouns in the
    first column to make the adjectives in the last column? ____

2. How many nouns in the first column end with **silent e**? ____
    Drop the ____ before you add **y**.

3. How many nouns follow the **1 + 1 + 1 spelling pattern**? ____
    Double the _____ before you add **y**.

> The ending **y** can be added to many nouns.
> Nouns with a **y** ending become **adjectives**, or words that describe something.

windy	lucky	smoky	grimy	funny
sandy	sleepy	shady	sunny	muddy
salty	icy	shiny	foggy	baggy

Practice the Words

A Use each clue to find a spelling word that fits in the boxes. Write the words.

1. bright and polished

2. has salt

3. misty

4. breezy

5. blocked from the sun

6. covered with mud

7. having good luck

8. slippery

9. hanging loosely

10. covered with dirt and grime

11. tired

12. full of smoke

13. makes you laugh

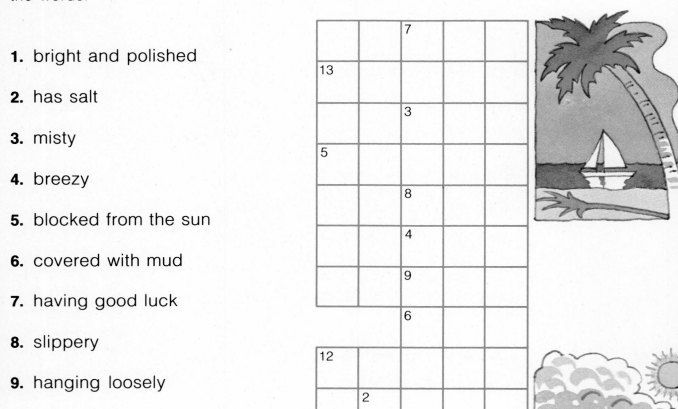

Look at the letters in the numbered boxes. Print each letter on the correct line to find out what an adjective is.

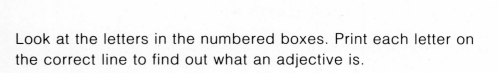

___ ___ ___ ___ ___ ___ ___   ___ ___ ___ ___   ___ ___ ___ ___
8   4   1   13 9   2   7   12 6   11 3   5   10 2   4

116

Proofreading

B Cross out the twelve misspelled words in these sentences. Write each word correctly.

The funey clown wore bagy pants and a grimey shirt. He had sleepey eyes and a shinny red nose painted on his face.

The morning will be fogy. We are lucky that the afternoon will be warm and suney.

Shadey trees grow along the sanddy banks of the mudey river. On a winddy day the water is icey.

1. _____

2. _____

3. _____

4. _____

5. _____

6. _____

7. _____

8. _____

9. _____

10. _____

11. _____

12. _____

Dictionary

Each dictionary entry tells the meaning, or definition, of the entry word.

C Write these words in alphabetical order. Look up each word in your spelling dictionary and complete the definition.

smoky   sunny   salty   lucky   sandy

1. _____ = having good _____

2. _____ = tasting of _____

3. _____ = full of _____

4. _____ = filled with _____

5. _____ = bright with _____

windy   lucky   smoky   grimy   funny

sandy   sleepy   shady   sunny   muddy

salty   icy   shiny   foggy   baggy

Build Word Power

Writing

Write new sentences using the **y** form of the underlined word.
Circle the word.

1. The <u>wind</u> is blowing today.

Today is (windy).

2. The room is filled with <u>smoke</u>.

3. You have <u>sand</u> on your feet.

4. Your shoes have <u>mud</u> on them.

5. There is <u>ice</u> on the sidewalk.

6. The popcorn has <u>salt</u> on it.

New Words   fur   rain   crunch   squeak

noise   grease   star   haste

Reach Out for New Words

A Write each new word in the correct column.

silent e	1 + 1 + 1	other
_____	_____	_____
_____	_____	_____
_____	_____	_____
_____	_____	_____
_____		_____

m	a	e	s	l	h	v	w	z	k	p	d	i	g	t	j	o	r	c	f	y	u	q	n	b	x
1	2	3	4	5	6	7	8	9	10	11	12	13	14	15	16	17	18	19	20	21	22	23	24	25	26

B Each number in this code stands for one letter of the alphabet.
Decode the missing words in the treasure hunt clues below. Each
word is the **y** form of a new word.

Begin on a ___ ___ ___ ___ ___ night. If there is a
........18..2..13..24..21

___ ___ ___ ___ ___ ___ sky, you may miss the clue in
.4..15..2..18..18..21

your umbrella!

Don't be ___ ___ ___ ___ ___ . You might not find the
........6..2..4..15..21

second clue in the pocket of a ___ ___ ___ ___ ___ coat!
............................20..22..18..18..21

Try not to be ___ ___ ___ ___ ___ . Look for the clue behind
..............24..17..13..4..21

the ___ ___ ___ ___ ___ ___ ___ bedroom door!
....4..23..22..3..2..10..21

Don't get your fingers ___ ___ ___ ___ ___ ___ looking!
.......................14..18..3..2..4..21

You will find the last clue under the jar of

___ ___ ___ ___ ___ ___ ___ peanut butter!
19..18..22..24..19..6..21

119

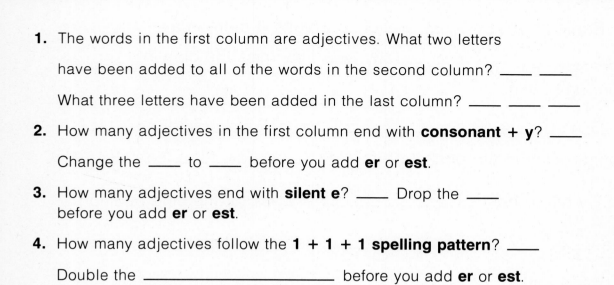

dark	darker	darkest	*darker*	*darkest*
small	smaller	smallest	*smaller*	*smallest*
happy	happier	happiest	*happier*	*happiest*
heavy	heavier	heaviest	*heavier*	*heaviest*
large	larger	largest	*larger*	*largest*
brave	braver	bravest	*braver*	*bravest*
big	bigger	biggest	*bigger*	*biggest*
hot	hotter	hottest	*hotter*	*hottest*

1. The words in the first column are adjectives. What two letters

   have been added to all of the words in the second column? ____ ____

   What three letters have been added in the last column? ____ ____ ____

2. How many adjectives in the first column end with **consonant + y**? ____

   Change the ____ to ____ before you add **er** or **est**.

3. How many adjectives end with **silent e**? ____ Drop the ____
   before you add **er** or **est**.

4. How many adjectives follow the **1 + 1 + 1 spelling pattern**? ____

   Double the _____ before you add **er** or **est**.

> The ending **er** can be added to many adjectives to mean **more**.
> The ending **est** can be added to many adjectives to mean **most**.

Practice the Words

A Find the missing letters in each word. Then write the word.

1. hottest    *hottest*

2. d__rk__r

3. l__r__e__

4. br__v__r

5. h____v__st

6. b__g__e__

7. sm__ll__r

8. l__r__e__t

9. d__r__e__t

10. h__pp__st

11. b__a__e__t

12. s__a__e__t

13. h__t__e__

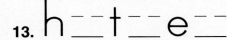

121

darker   darkest   braver   bravest
smaller   smallest   happier   happiest
heavier   heaviest   bigger   biggest
larger   largest   hotter   hottest

B Complete each phrase with the **er** or **est** form of the given word.
Use **er** to compare two people or things. Use **est** to compare three
or more people or things.

1. heavy _____ of the five boxes

2. dark   _____ hair than yours

3. brave _____ than Sir Richard

4. big   _____ than my dog

5. large _____ elephant in the jungle

6. hot   _____ day of the summer

7. big   _____ house in town

8. small _____ kitten in the litter

9. heavy _____ than a brick

Dictionary

C The **er** and **est** forms of a word are not listed as entry words in the
dictionary. They are often found at the end of the entry for a base
word. Write the entry word for each of these adjectives.

1. heavier _____   5. smaller _____

2. darkest _____   6. bravest _____

3. hotter   _____   7. biggest _____

4. happiest _____   8. larger   _____

Writing

Write an answer for each question about the clowns. Use the **er** or **est** spelling word that means the same as the underlined words at the left of each sentence.

Grumpy   Rocko   Pinky

1. most big   Who has the ___ hat?

_____

_ _

_____

2. more happy   Which clown is ___ than Rocko?

_____

_ _

_____

3. most heavy   Which clown is ___ ?

_____

_ _

_____

4. most dark   Who has the ___ hair?

_____

_ _

_____

5. more small   Which clown is ___ than Rocko?

_____

_ _

_____

Reach Out for New Words

A Write the **er** form of each new word. Watch out for **silent e**, **consonant + y**, and **1 + 1 + 1** words.

1. _____

2. _____

3. _____

4. _____

5. _____

6. _____

7. _____

8. _____

9. _____

B Write the word that means the opposite of each word or phrase. Use the **est** form of one of the new words.

1. driest

2. most bumpy

3. hardest to do

4. wildest

5. happiest

6. busiest

7. oldest

8. narrowest

9. most full of food

wear	*wear*
bear	*bear*
pear	*pear*
tear	*tear*
earn	*earn*
learn	*learn*
earth	*earth*
heard	*heard*
early	*early*
near	*near*
hear	*hear*
year	*year*
fear	*fear*
dear	*dear*
clear	*clear*

1. What three letters do you see in every word? ___ ___ ___

2. In how many words do the letters **ear** sound like the word **air**? ___

3. In how many words do the letters **ear** sound like **ur** in the word **turn**? ___

4. In how many words do the letters **ear** sound like **eer** in the word **deer**? ___

Many words are spelled with the letters **ear**.
The letters **ear** may have different sounds.

wear	tear	earth	near	fear
bear	earn	heard	hear	dear
pear	learn	early	year	clear

Practice the Words

A Write the spelling words that complete these sentences.

1. Worms live in the _____ .

2. I can see through this _____ glass.

3. Did you _____ that _____ growl?

4. Rob wants to _____ money for a new bike.

5. Kathy _____ an airplane fly over the house.

6. I will get up _____ tomorrow morning.

7. Don't _____ your good shirt to the picnic.

8. Next _____ I will _____ how to swim.

9. Did Mike _____ his jacket when he fell?

10. My _____ friend Kerry is moving _____ us.

11. Ben tried to get over his _____ of spiders.

Proofreading

B Cross out each misspelled word. Write the word correctly.

1. *Last yere I learned not to feer the water.*

_____   _____

2. *Tim herd a bear neer our cabin.*

_____   _____

3. *Erly this morning the sky was cleer.*

_____   _____

4. *The roots of the pare tree are deep in the erth.*

_____   _____

C Write funny answers for these clues. Use two rhyming spelling words for each answer.

1. what 364 days are _____ *near* _____ a _____ *year* _____

2. a rip made by a large furry animal   a _____   _____

3. take a lesson to make money   _____   to   _____

4. put a fruit on your head   _____   a   _____

5. listen to someone you love   _____   a   _____

wear	tear	earth	near	fear
bear	earn	heard	hear	dear
pear	learn	early	year	clear

Build Word Power

Look at the first pair of words in each row. In what way do these words go together? Write a spelling word that makes the second pair of words go together in the same way as the first pair.

1. **puppy** is to **dog**   as   **cub** is to   _____

2. **fish** is to **water**   as   **worm** is to   _____

3. **eye** is to **see**   as   **ear** is to   _____

4. **glass** is to **break**   as   **paper** is to   _____

5. **games** are to **play**   as   **lessons** are to   _____

6. **flower** is to **rose**   as   **fruit** is to   _____

7. **food** is to **tasted**   as   **sound** is to   _____

8. **there** is to **here**   as   **far** is to   _____

9. **purse** is to **carry**   as   **shirt** is to   _____

10. **day** is to **week**   as   **month** is to   _____

128

Search for new words!
Follow the directions below.

Reach Out for New Words

A In this puzzle, each number is written twice. Find the **ear** word in each pair of numbers. Connect the dots that go with **ear** words.

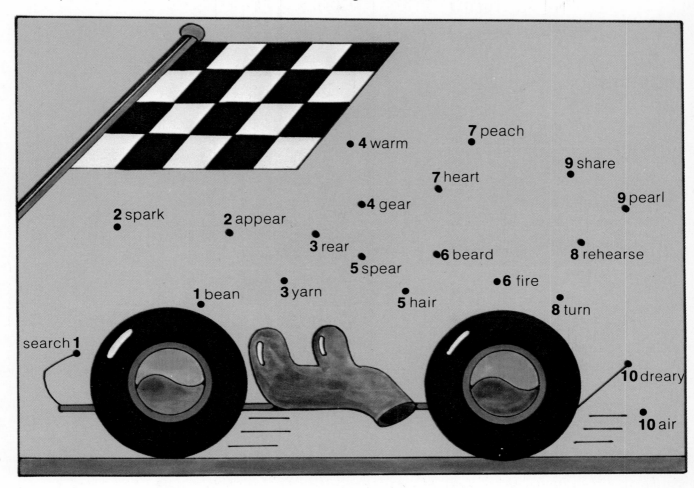

7 peach

4 warm

9 share

7 heart

9 pearl

4 gear

2 spark

2 appear

3 rear

6 beard

8 rehearse

5 spear

6 fire

1 bean

3 yarn

5 hair

8 turn

search **1**

10 dreary

10 air

B Unscramble each group of letters to make one of the **ear** words from the puzzle.

1. erra _____

2. drabe _____

3. plare _____

4. chears _____

5. prapea _____

6. thare _____

7. yarder _____

8. rega _____

9. sheerear _____

10. prase _____

high	*high*
sigh	*sigh*
thigh	*thigh*
night	*night*
sight	*sight*
fight	*fight*
right	*right*
light	*light*
tight	*tight*
might	*might*
bright	*bright*
flight	*flight*
tonight	*tonight*
frighten	*frighten*
lightning	*lightning*

1. What three letters do you see in every word? ____ ____ ____

2. Which one of these letters do you hear when you say each word? ____

3. Which two of these letters are silent? ____ ____

Many words are spelled with the letters **igh**.
The letters **g** and **h** are silent.

Practice the Words

Proofreading

A Write the spelling words that answer each question.

1. Which three words have two syllables?

_____ _____ _____

_____ _____ _____

2. Which three words end with **h**?

_____ _____ _____

_____ _____ _____

3. Which eight words have five letters?

_____ _____ _____

_____ _____ _____

_____ _____ _____

_____ _____

4. Which five words have more than five letters?

_____ _____ _____

_____ _____

_____ _____

B Complete each phrase with a spelling word.

1. a _____ mountain

2. late at _____

3. _____ an enemy

4. an airplane _____

5. with all your _____

6. a _____ of relief

7. _____ shoes

8. thunder and _____

Dictionary

Some words have more than one meaning, or definition, listed in the dictionary. Each definition is given a number.

right (rīt) *adjective* ①correct or true [That is the *right* way to go.] ②opposite of left [Raise your *right* hand.]   definition numbers

C   Complete each sentence with a word from the box. Look up each word in your spelling dictionary. Write the number of the meaning that was used in the sentence.

right   light   bright   sight

1. Do you know the _____*right*_____ answer?   1

2. We should buy a _____ for this dark room.   _____

3. The waterfall was a beautiful _____ .   _____

4. Ann throws the ball with her _____ hand.   _____

5. That _____ boy answered every question.   _____

6. The blind man regained his _____ .   _____

7. The candle gave off a soft _____ .   _____

8. That spotlight is very _____ .   _____

high	night	right	might	tonight
sigh	sight	light	bright	frighten
thigh	fight	tight	flight	lightning

Build Word Power

Make new words by adding endings to your spelling words. You do
not need to change the base word in any way before you add an ending.

s   ed   ing   er   est

high

_____

- - - - - - - - - -

_____

- - - - - - - - - -

_____

night

_____

- - - - - - - - - -

_____

bright

_____

- - - - - - - - - -

_____

- - - - - - - - - -

_____

sigh

_____

- - - - - - - - - -

_____

- - - - - - - - - -

_____

fight

_____

- - - - - - - - - -

_____

- - - - - - - - - -

_____

light

_____

- - - - - - - - - -

_____

- - - - - - - - - -

_____

- - - - - - - - - -

_____

frighten

_____

- - - - - - - - - -

_____

- - - - - - - - - -

_____

Reach Out for New Words

A Beginning with the spelling word **light**, follow the directions to make the five new **igh** words.

Look at the word **light**.   **light**

1. Add **s** to the beginning.

2. Change **s** to **twi**.

3. Change **twi** to **de**.
   Add **ed** to the end.

4. Take away **ed**.
   Change **del** to **midn**.

5. Change **midn** to **he**.

Proofreading

B Cross out five misspelled words. Write the words correctly.

> *It was twiligt when a sleight
> rain began. Bill was delited
> to hear the raindrops on the roof.
> The weatherman had said there would be a
> bad storm. The storm would be at its
> hight around midnite.*

1. _____   4. _____

2. _____   5. _____

3. _____

Using Review Words

A Look at the first pair of words in each row. In what way do these words go together? Write a spelling word that makes the second pair of words go together in the same way as the first pair.

1. **storm** is to **stormy**   as   **wind** is to   _____

2. **bravest** is to **brave**   as   **largest** is to   _____

3. **swim** is to **swimmer**   as   **win** is to   _____

4. **dance** is to **dancer**   as   **skate** is to   _____

5. **stormy** is to **storm**   as   **windy** is to   _____

6. **windy** is to **windier**   as   **heavy** is to   _____

7. **swimmer** is to **swim**   as   **winner** is to   _____

8. **happiest** is to **happy**   as   **funniest** is to   _____

Proofreading

B Cross out each misspelled word. Write the correct spelling.

1. *Verry few skaters were on the icey pond.*

_____   _____

_____   _____

2. *I can lern to spell everey word right.*

_____   _____

_____   _____

3. *The stoarm blew down the largist tree.*

_____   _____

_____   _____

C Find the word from the box that goes in each blank.

story	*hear*	*right*	*summer*	*word*
pitcher	*light*	*wear*	*high*	*biggest*

1. a spelling _____

2. _____ your coat

3. baseball _____

4. write a _____

5. my _____ hand

6. the _____ piece

7. _____ as a feather

8. _____ in the air

9. hot _____ day

10. _____ a noise

137

Using More Review Words

A Follow these directions.

1. Put a ☐ around each **silent e** word.
Write the **er** form of these words.

2. Put a ⬭ around each **consonant + y** word.
Write the **er** form of these words.

3. Put a * after each **1 + 1 + 1 word.**
Write the **er** form of these words.

4. Write the **er** form of the four words you have left.

1. shop		**9.** small	
2. ☐ brave	*braver*	**10.** swim	
3. dark		**11.** carry	
4. lead		**12.** bake	
5. hot		**13.** copy	
6. fly		**14.** wipe	
7. large		**15.** work	
8. dance			

B Three words in each row follow the same spelling pattern. One does not. Find that word. Be ready to tell why it does not belong.

1. sleepiest   darkest   windiest   luckiest

2. saddest   hottest   biggest   largest

3. bear   earn   clear   fight

4. world   herd   person   very

5. smoky   shady   salty   shiny

6. swim   worm   shop   win

7. right   large   bright   high

C Look at the first pair of words in each row. Write a word from the box that makes the second pair of words go together in the same way.

| sandy | sight | painter | night |
| horn | winter | bright | fork |

1. **light** is to **day**   as   **dark** is to _____

2. **beat** is to **drum**   as   **blow** is to _____

3. **pen** is to **writer**   as   **brush** is to _____

4. **soup** is to **spoon**   as   **meat** is to _____

5. **lawn** is to **grassy**   as   **beach** is to _____

6. **ears** are to **hearing**   as   **eyes** are to _____

7. **dark** is to **light**   as   **dull** is to _____

8. **hot** is to **summer**   as   **cold** is to _____

melted	from	minutes	always
month	drift	warning	during
also	flood	forecast	evening
warm	burst	beautiful	almost

Prewriting. Prewriting means getting ready to write. You must plan and organize your ideas before you begin writing.

Use Prewriting Skills

Use the spelling words to plan a report about the weather.

1. What two words can you use to describe the weather?

   _____   _____

   _____   _____

2. What two words remind you of snow?

   _____   _____

   _____   _____

3. What is caused by too much rain or melted snow? _____

4. What two words are measures of time?

   _____   _____

   _____   _____

5. What word means to tell about something before it happens?

   _____

   _____

Now Think

Pretend you are a weather reporter. Will you tell about an awful storm or about a beautiful day? Think about a time when the weather was really special for some reason. What kinds of things happened because of the weather? On your own paper, write some ideas for a weather report.

Writing. A story may be made up of paragraphs. A paragraph is a group of sentences about one idea. Each sentence in a paragraph tells about that main idea. The sentences must be arranged in an order that makes sense.

Use Writing Skills

A Practice writing topic sentences that tell a main idea. Write two different endings for each sentence starter below.

1. Today's weather was the ____ .

2. Everyone was surprised by ____ .

Sometimes two parts of the same sentence are incorrectly separated by a period. One part is not a complete thought. It must be joined to the rest of the sentence.

Incomplete: I ran into the house. Because it started to rain.

Complete: I ran into the house because it started to rain.

B Make each word group into a complete sentence. Write the sentences on your own paper.

1. a beautiful summer day

2. almost melted

3. a sudden burst of rain

4. earlier this evening

5. swept away by flood water

6. during a winter storm

7. a few minutes later

8. a warning to drivers

Now Write   Write a first draft of your paragraph about the weather. Follow the directions below.

1. Begin with a topic sentence. You may want to use one of the topic sentences from Exercise A.

2. Try to use some of the sentences from Exercise B. Put your sentences in an order that makes sense. First tell about the weather. Next, tell what happens because of the weather. Then give a forecast of the coming weather.

Revising. Revising means changing parts of your first draft to make it better. First read your draft aloud to make sure that you like the way your ideas sound. Then proofread your writing to find mistakes in capitalization, punctuation, and spelling.

Use Revising and Proofreading Skills

A Revise the ideas in the report below. After you have marked the changes, copy the revised story on your own paper.

1. Underline a sentence in the first paragraph that would be better at the end of the story. It tells about tomorrow's weather.
2. Find a sentence that has a missing word. Find another sentence that is an incomplete thought. Mark each place with a carat (∧) and add the needed words.
3. In the third paragraph, cross out a sentence that doesn't tell about the main idea.

Last night's snowstorm took everyone by surprise. The snow is expected to melt by tomorrow. Snow has never fallen in Janesville so late in the spring. May is the month when winter is supposed to over!

Yesterday was beautiful. The sun felt warm and spring was in the air. A few flowers were beginning to bud. Chirping in the trees. Children carried their jackets home from school in the afternoon.

During the night, though, winter came back without warning. Snow and ice covered the ground. Since no one was ready to clear the roads this morning, school buses couldn't travel and schools were closed. Janesville bought two new school buses last year.

B Practice your proofreading skills on the story below.

1. Cross out eight misspelled words and write them correctly on the lines.
2. Circle and correct six capitalization mistakes.
3. Circle and correct four punctuation errors.

Remember
- A sentence begins with a capital letter and ends with a period.
- The names of particular places are capitalized.
- A period is not used to separate parts of one thought.

Today was the hottest day of the summer in downtown columbus. July is allways a warm mounth in our City, but today's heat was awful. The sun beat down frum the cloudless sky. The streets were quiet. Because no one wanted to be out in the bright sun. A boy came out of the Favorite flavor Factory with an ice cream cone in his hand. Two minits later, his ice cream had meltid. And dripped on the hot sidewalk. Durring the afternoon, a few clouds drifted across the sky? They didn't make it any cooler, though. The weather forcast for tomorrow is not much better, it will be all most as hot as today.

1. _____   5. _____

2. _____   6. _____

3. _____   7. _____

4. _____   8. _____

Now Revise   Read the first draft of your story. Is each sentence about the main idea? Are the sentences arranged in an order that makes sense?

Proofread and correct mistakes in capitalization, punctuation, and spelling. Write your final copy in your best handwriting.

A Writer's Journal

UNIT FOUR

Has a poem ever made you think, "This is how I feel" or "*I've* done these things"? A poem may help you remember happy times or sad times you may have had with a friend or with your family. That's why reading poetry is one way to get ideas for writing in your journal.

Read this poem. Try to picture in your mind what the two friends are doing. Then discuss the questions with your class.

SECRET TALK

I have a friend
and sometimes we meet
and greet each other
without a word.

We walk through a field
and stalk a bird
and chew a blade of
pungent grass.

We let time pass
for a golden hour
while we twirl a flower
of Queen Ann's lace
or find a lion's face
shaped in a cloud
that's drifting, sifting
across the sky.

There's no need to say,
"It's been a fine day"
when we say goodbye:
when we say goodbye
we just wave a hand
and we understand.

—EVE MERRIAM

Talking About the Poem

1. Where are the two friends playing? What are some of the things the two friends did?

2. Why don't the friends need to say that it had been a fine day when they say goodbye?

3. What is "secret talk"?

Writing in Your Journal

The poem talks about two friends. Maybe this poem has helped you remember a special friend and has given you an idea to write about in your journal. If you need help getting started, here are some other ideas you might use.

1. Write about some special looks, actions, or words that you and a friend use and understand.

2. Write about a special time that you and a friend had together. Describe where you were and what you did.

Building a Personal Word List

You have been collecting your misspelled words and writing them on your personal word list. How can you learn to spell these words? You might try one of these ways:

1. Look carefully at the words on your list. Do any of them look like words you already know how to spell? For example, knowing how to spell **grimy** may help you spell **slimy**.

2. Look for patterns. Do any of your words have spelling patterns you know? For example, you might notice that **high, bright,** and **lightning** have the same **igh** pattern. Practice spelling the words as a group.

wrist	*wrist*
wrong	*wrong*
wreck	*wreck*
wren	*wren*
wrapper	*wrapper*
knee	*knee*
know	*know*
knew	*knew*
knuckle	*knuckle*
knotted	*knotted*
climb	*climb*
comb	*comb*
crumb	*crumb*
lamb	*lamb*
limb	*limb*

1. What silent letter begins each word in the first group? ＿＿

2. What silent letter begins each word in the second group? ＿＿

3. What silent letter ends each word in the third group? ＿＿

Some words are spelled with a silent letter.

Practice the Words

A Write the spelling words that complete this story.

                    Carol didn't _____ how much fun her uncle's

farm could be. She fed a young _____ milk from a

bottle. She gave a baby duck a _____ of bread.

                    Next, Carol was allowed to _____ on a pony's

back and take a ride. Her uncle told her to wrap the reins around her hand.

She learned to guide the pony by moving her _____ or

her _____. At first Carol did it all _____ .

She thought she would _____ the corral! Soon

she _____ what to do. When the ride was over,

she _____ the reins around a fence post. Her uncle

let her _____ the pony's mane. Then she fed the pony

pieces of apple.

B Write the spelling word that rhymes with the clue word.

1. hen   _____
2. spotted   _____
3. go   _____
4. slam   _____
5. trim   _____

6. two   _____
7. gum   _____
8. snapper   _____
9. time   _____
10. buckle   _____

Dictionary

The dictionary gives many clues to explain the meanings of words.
The dictionary may give a sample sentence to make the meaning clearer.
The dictionary may give a picture of the word.

know (nō) *verb* to be aware of; realize [Does he *know* what happened?] —**knew, known, know′ ing**

lamb (lam) *noun* a young sheep. —*plural* **lambs**

C Look up each word in your spelling dictionary. Write it in the correct column.

know   *limb*   *knee*   *wrong*   *wreck*   *wren*
lamb   *comb*   *wrapper*   *wrist*   *climb*   *knuckle*

Sentence Clue

know

Picture Clue

lamb

148

wrist   wren   know   knotted   crumb
wrong   wrapper   knew   climb   lamb
wreck   knee   knuckle   comb   limb

Build Word Power

Follow the directions to change each clue word into a spelling word.

Clue Word	Change	Spelling Word
		limb
lime	**e** to **b**	
twist	**tw** to **wr**	
trapper	**t** to **w**	
crust	**st** to **mb**	
blew	**bl** to **kn**	
wrote	**te** to **ng**	
click	**ck** to **mb**	

Clue Word		Spelling Word
knot	*t to w*	know
lamp		lamb
free		knee
check		wreck
chuckle		knuckle

149

Search for new words!
Follow the directions below.

Reach Out for New Words

A Find the correct path through this maze. You are on the right path if you pass words that have a silent letter. Write the eight words from your path.

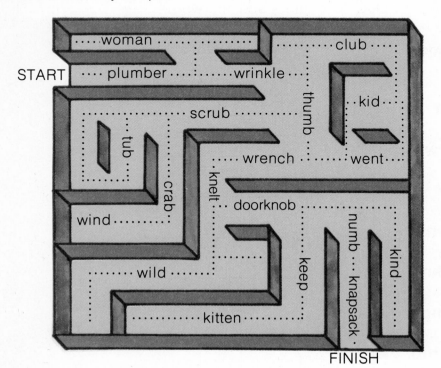

1. _____
2. _____
3. _____
4. _____
5. _____
6. _____
7. _____
8. _____

B Find the misspelled word in each group. Write the word correctly.

1. crumb
wrong
plumer
knew

_____

2. rinkle
comb
wreck
knapsack

_____

3. wrong
doornob
lamb
know

_____

4. wreck
know
wrist
thum

_____

5. wrapper
knotted
num
knee

_____

6. rench
limb
knelt
climb

_____

un +	true	=	untrue	*untrue*
un +	fair	=	unfair	*unfair*
un +	kind	=	unkind	*unkind*
un +	wise	=	unwise	*unwise*
un +	safe	=	unsafe	*unsafe*
un +	tie	=	untie	*untie*
un +	lock	=	unlock	*unlock*
un +	cover	=	uncover	*uncover*
un +	wrap	=	unwrap	*unwrap*
un +	plug	=	unplug	*unplug*
un +	pack	=	unpack	*unpack*
un +	button	=	unbutton	*unbutton*
un +	willing	=	unwilling	*unwilling*
un +	even	=	uneven	*uneven*
un +	opened	=	unopened	*unopened*

A **prefix** is a group of letters added to the beginning of a word to change its meaning.

1. What prefix was added to each base word to make the words in the last column? ____ ____
2. Was the spelling of the base word changed when the prefix was added? ____

The prefix **un** means <u>not</u> or <u>opposite of</u>.
Do not change the spelling of the base word when you add the prefix **un**.

   un + happy = unhappy or **not happy**

untrue   unwise   unlock   unplug   unwilling

unfair   unsafe   uncover   unpack   uneven

unkind   untie   unwrap   unbutton   unopened

Practice the Words

A Use each clue to find a spelling word that fits in the puzzle.

Across
2. to take the lid off
3. not playing by the rules
4. to pull out a plug
7. ____ your shoelaces
9. ____ the door
10. dangerous
11. not nice

Down
1. to loosen buttons
2. false
3. to take clothes from a suitcase
5. closed
6. foolish
8. to take off wrapping paper

B In each sentence, find the base form of one of your spelling words. Add the prefix **un** to the word. You will make a word with the opposite meaning.

1. Bill told a true story.

2. Julie said the test was fair.

3. We should cover the wet clay.

4. Remember to tie your shoe.

5. The hem of the skirt was even.

6. I am willing to wash the dishes.

Dictionary

Many words with prefixes are listed as entry words in the dictionary.

C Write your spelling words in alphabetical order. When words begin with the same letter, look at the next letter to find the alphabetical order. For some words, you will need to look at the third, fourth, or fifth letter.

unload

unlock

unlucky

1. _____

2. _____

3. _____

4. _____

5. _____

6. _____

7. _____

8. _____

9. _____

10. _____

11. _____

12. _____

13. _____

14. _____

15. _____

153

untrue   unwise   unlock   unplug   unwilling

unfair   unsafe   uncover   unpack   uneven

unkind   untie   unwrap   unbutton   unopened

Build Word Power

Find the spelling word that completes each sentence. Change the spelling word to a form that will make sense in the sentence. Then write the word. You may add endings such as **s**, **ed**, or **ing**. You may also take off the prefix **un**. Watch out for **silent e** and **1 + 1 + 1** words.

1. Sue unpack her suitcase when she got home.

unpacked

2. It is unwise to look both ways before you cross the street.

3. Becky enjoys unwrap her birthday gifts.

4. Bill unbutton his coat when the cold wind began to blow.

5. Betty uncover the pot and cooks the rice.

New Words

unhurt	unhealthy	unafraid	unable
unbroken	unfasten	unequal	unripe

Reach Out for New Words

A Unscramble each new word. First find the prefix **un**, which is not scrambled. Then unscramble the rest of the letters. Write each new word.

1. nesuntaf _____

2. lunaque _____

3. truhun _____

4. blunea _____

5. preiun _____

6. teaunhylh _____

7. draifuna _____

8. nebkunor _____

B Write the new **un** word that means the same as each word or phrase below.

1. sick _____

2. all in one piece _____

3. to open buttons _____

4. not able to _____

5. brave _____

6. not the same _____

7. not ready to eat _____

8. not in pain _____

re	+	write	=	rewrite	*rewrite*
re	+	fill	=	refill	*refill*
re	+	read	=	reread	*reread*
re	+	paint	=	repaint	*repaint*
re	+	pay	=	repay	*repay*
re	+	wind	=	rewind	*rewind*
re	+	visit	=	revisit	*revisit*
re	+	heat	=	reheat	*reheat*
re	+	teach	=	reteach	*reteach*
re	+	build	=	rebuild	*rebuild*
re	+	tell	=	retell	*retell*
re	+	turn	=	return	*return*
re	+	take	=	retake	*retake*
re	+	print	=	reprint	*reprint*
re	+	place	=	replace	*replace*

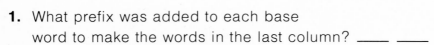

1. What prefix was added to each base word to make the words in the last column? ____ ____

2. Was the spelling of the base word changed before the prefix was added? ____

The prefix **re** means <u>again</u> or <u>back</u>.
Do not change the spelling of the base word when you add the prefix **re**.
   re + paint = repaint or **paint again**

156

Practice the Words

A Change the underlined words in each sentence to one spelling word.

1. Please <u>fill</u> my glass <u>again</u>. _____

2. Ms. Gomez will <u>teach</u> the lesson <u>again</u>. _____

3. Will you <u>tell</u> my favorite story <u>again</u>? _____

4. Ken should <u>pay back</u> the quarter he owes you. _____

5. Val wants to <u>paint</u> her room <u>again</u>. _____

6. They are going to <u>build</u> the clubhouse <u>again</u>. _____

7. Should I <u>take</u> your picture <u>again</u>? _____

8. Did you <u>write</u> your story <u>again</u>? _____

9. I will <u>heat</u> the soup <u>again</u> for lunch. _____

10. Today we must <u>turn back</u> our library books. _____

11. Jerry will <u>wind</u> the toy robot <u>again</u>. _____

12. Our class will <u>visit</u> the museum <u>again</u>. _____

rewrite	repaint	revisit	rebuild	retake
refill	repay	reheat	retell	reprint
reread	rewind	reteach	return	replace

B Look at each word. If it is spelled correctly, draw a ☺. If it is misspelled, write the word correctly.

1. retell _____

2. reheet _____

3. replase _____

4. rewrite _____

5. rebild _____

6. revissit _____

7. repprint _____

8. refil _____

9. rereed _____

10. reteach _____

11. retern _____

12. repay _____

Dictionary

C The words below are dictionary guide words. Write the spelling words that would appear on the same page.

1. retain   revote

2. rewash   rezone

3. repaid   rerun

Make four new words from each base word below. Add the prefix **re** or one of the endings shown in the train. Sometimes you may want to use both a prefix and an ending. Watch out for **silent e** words.

re | Base Word | s | es | ed | ing | er

write

rewrite
writer
writing
rewrites

paint

teach

build

fill

read

Reach Out for New Words

A Print the **re** form of the new word that fits in each shape.

1.

2.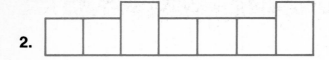

3.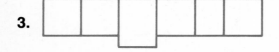

4.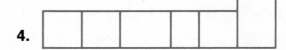

5.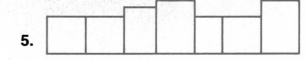

6.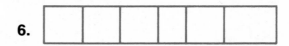

B Write the **re** form of each new word in alphabetical order. Then look up each word in your spelling dictionary and complete the definition.

_____

1. _____ = to _____ back

2. _____ = to _____ _____ again

3. _____ = to make _____

4. _____ = to make _____ or _____ again

5. _____ = to _____ over again

6. _____ = to go _____ or _____ again

let +	us	=	let's	*let's*
are +	not	=	aren't	*aren't*
did +	not	=	didn't	*didn't*
do +	not	=	don't	*don't*
was +	not	=	wasn't	*wasn't*
were +	not	=	weren't	*weren't*
I +	have	=	I've	*I've*
you +	have	=	you've	*you've*
that +	is	=	that's	*that's*
how +	is	=	how's	*how's*
what +	is	=	what's	*what's*
who +	is	=	who's	*who's*
he +	will	=	he'll	*he'll*
we +	will	=	we'll	*we'll*
we +	are	=	we're	*we're*

1. The words in the last column are **contractions**.
   Each contraction is made from how many words? ____
2. Were any letters left out when the words were put together? _____
3. In each contraction, an **apostrophe** takes the
   place of one or more letters. Draw an apostrophe. ____

A **contraction** is made from two words.
When the two words are put together, an **apostrophe** (')
takes the place of one or more letters.

let's	don't	I've	how's	he'll
aren't	wasn't	you've	what's	we'll
didn't	weren't	that's	who's	we're

Practice the Words

A Write the contractions in alphabetical order in the first column.
Answer the questions at the top of the second and third columns.

	Contraction	What two words is it made from?	What letter(s) does the ' replace?
1.	*aren't*	*are not*	*o*
2.			
3.			
4.	*he'll*		
5.			
6.			
7.			
8.			
9.			
10.			*wi*
11.			
12.			
13.			
14.			
15.			

B Match the words with the correct endings to make contractions. Write each contraction you make.

1. what

2. do

3. are   ___ 's

4. how   ___ n't

5. you   ___ 've

6. I

7. were

1. _____

2. _____

3. _____

4. _____

5. _____

6. _____

7. _____

C Read each sentence. Find each pair of words that can be made into a contraction. Write the contraction.

1. We are sure we will enjoy the game.

_____   _____

_____   _____

2. Carol was not singing because she did not know the song.

_____   _____

_____   _____

3. That is the record he will bring to the party.

_____   _____

_____   _____

4. Let us ask Mary who is going to the game.

_____   _____

_____   _____

let's   don't   I've   how's   he'll
aren't   wasn't   you've   what's   we'll
didn't   weren't   that's   who's   we're

Build Word Power

Writing

Write a sentence to answer each question. In your answer, use the contraction in parentheses. Remember to start each sentence with a capital letter.

1. What is Fred going to do this weekend?   (he'll)

_____

_ _

_____

2. What books have you read this year?   (I've)

_____

_ _

_____

3. When will we pick up Jean at the airport?   (we'll)

_____

_ _

_____

4. What shall we have for dinner?   (let's)

_____

_ _

_____

5. Why didn't you finish your homework?   (don't)

_____

_ _

_____

6. How many cookies are in the cookies jar?   (aren't)

_____

_ _

_____

New Words   couldn't   shouldn't   hasn't   doesn't   hadn't
                I'd   you'd   they'd   she'd   we'd

Reach Out for New Words

A Write the contraction for each pair of words. Each contraction
should fit in the boxes. An apostrophe fills one box.

1. she would

2. they would

3. does not

4. you would

5. could not

6. I would

7. has not

8. we would

9. had not

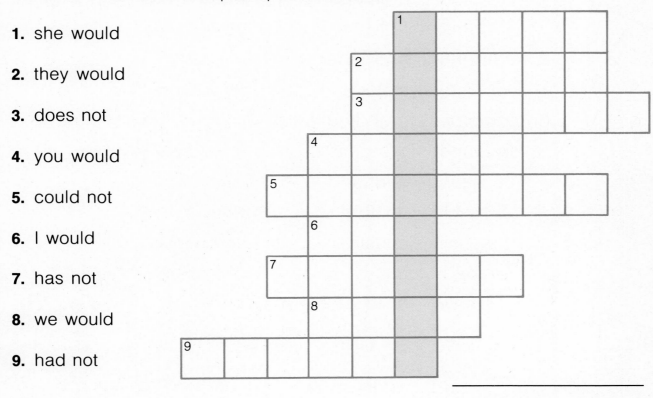

What contraction do you see in the colored boxes? _____

Proofreading

B Cross out each misspelled word. Write the word correctly.

1. They'ed already finished the job.   _____

2. I thought youd like a snack.   _____

3. That lamp dosen't work.   _____

4. Could't we wait inside?   _____

5. Here's the book Id like to read.   _____

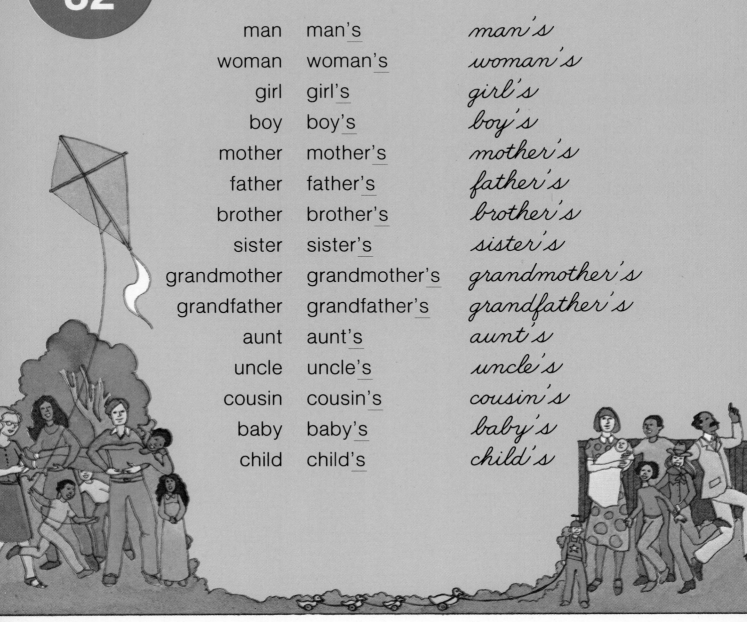

man	man's	*man's*
woman	woman's	*woman's*
girl	girl's	*girl's*
boy	boy's	*boy's*
mother	mother's	*mother's*
father	father's	*father's*
brother	brother's	*brother's*
sister	sister's	*sister's*
grandmother	grandmother's	*grandmother's*
grandfather	grandfather's	*grandfather's*
aunt	aunt's	*aunt's*
uncle	uncle's	*uncle's*
cousin	cousin's	*cousin's*
baby	baby's	*baby's*
child	child's	*child's*

The **possessive form** of a noun shows that something belongs to someone.

1. Each noun in the first column names a _____.
2. The nouns in the second column are in the possessive form. What was added to each noun? ____
3. Was the spelling of the base word changed before **'s** was added? _____

Make the **possessive form** of a noun by adding **'s**.
Do not change the spelling of the base word before adding **'s**.
> **That car belongs to my father.**
> **That is my father's car.**

166

Writing

A Choose something from the box that can belong to each person listed below. Then write a phrase using both words. Use the correct possessive form for each person.

football	house	pen	kitten	desk
balloon	dog	ring	socks	shorts
radio	hat	jacket	boat	car

1. aunt   *my aunt's kitten*

2. boy

3. cousin

4. woman

5. uncle

6. mother

7. man

8. sister

9. father

10. girl

11. baby

12. brother

13. grandmother

14. child

15. grandfather

B Find the misspelled word in each group. Write the word correctly.

1. woman's
father's
brother's
cuosin's

_____
_ _ _ _ _ _ _ _ _ _
_____

2. mother's
babie's
sister's
girl's

_____
_ _ _ _ _ _ _ _ _ _
_____

3. aunt's
uncle's
mans'
boy's

_____
_ _ _ _ _ _ _ _ _ _
_____

4. uncel's
grandfather's
aunt's
mother's

_____
_ _ _ _ _ _ _ _ _ _
_____

5. father's
boy's
sister's
chileds'

_____
_ _ _ _ _ _ _ _ _ _
_____

6. girl's
grandmother's
bruther's
woman's

_____
_ _ _ _ _ _ _ _ _ _
_____

C Words are written in two directions in this puzzle. → ↓ Find and circle the base form of nine spelling words. Then write the possessive form of each.

```
g i r l g f g
r c z h x a r
a u n t b t a
n k f j w h n
d b l v t e d
m o t h e r f
o y b m a b a
t d m g r l t
h w o m a n h
e n h p i q e
r s i s t e r
```

1. _____
2. _____
3. _____
4. _____
5. _____
6. _____
7. _____
8. _____
9. _____

man's	mother's	grandmother's	cousin's
woman's	father's	grandfather's	baby's
girl's	brother's	aunt's	child's
boy's	sister's	uncle's	

Build Word Power

Rewrite each sentence using the possessive form of the underlined word.

1. This dog belongs to my <u>sister</u>.

This is my sister's dog.

2. This glove belongs to the <u>boy</u>.

3. Mr. Kim is a neighbor of my <u>uncle</u>.

4. Tess is a friend of my <u>brother</u>.

5. Mrs. Sill is the teacher of my <u>cousin</u>.

6. These golf clubs belong to my <u>aunt</u>.

New Words   doctor   nurse   niece   nephew
neighbor   daughter   lady   friend

Reach Out for New Words

A Add the missing letters to make the new words.
Write the word. Then write its possessive form.

1. ___ ur ___ ___

2. ___ eigh ___ ___ ___

3. ___ ___ dy

4. ___ ie ___ ___

5. ___ ___ ie ___ ___

6. ___ ___ ___ ___ or

7. ___ ___ ph ___ ___

8. ___ augh ___ ___ ___

B Write a phrase using each pair of words. Use the possessive form
of each new word.

1. lady   umbrella   *the lady's umbrella*

2. nurse   uniform   _____

3. doctor   office   _____

170

apple	*apple*
puzzle	*puzzle*
little	*little*
bottle	*bottle*
rattle	*rattle*
middle	*middle*
wiggle	*wiggle*
bubble	*bubble*
puddle	*puddle*
juggle	*juggle*
scribble	*scribble*
cattle	*cattle*
nibble	*nibble*
riddle	*riddle*
giggle	*giggle*

1. How many words have the letters **tt**? ____ **gg**? ____
                                     bb? ____ **dd**? ____

2. What other double letters do you see? _____ _____

3. Are the double letters in each word vowels or consonants? _____

4. What two letters come after each double consonant? _____

Many words have a **double consonant** followed by **le**.

171

A Write the word that fits each clue.

1. I'm the center.

2. I'm all wet and shaped like ⬚⬚⬚⬚⬚ .

3. I float through the air.

4. I'm very small.

5. Can you find an answer to me?

6. Babies like to play with me.

7. I'm a cute laugh.

8. Put me together to make this shape: ⬚⬚⬚⬚⬚ .

9. I'm a little bite.

10. I'm shaped like ⬚⬚⬚⬚ .

11. You write me and I'm shaped like ⬚⬚⬚⬚⬚⬚⬚ .

12. I'm made of glass.

13. I'm the way a worm moves.

apple	bottle	wiggle	juggle	nibble
puzzle	rattle	bubble	scribble	riddle
little	middle	puddle	cattle	giggle

B Complete the funny answers for these clues with two rhyming spelling words.

1. shake the cows _____ the _____

2. twist and turn when you laugh _____ and _____

3. the joke in the center _____ in the _____

4. chew on messy writing _____ the _____

apple   puzzle   little   bottle
bubble   puddle   juggle

C Write the words from the box in alphabetical order. Then look up each word in your spelling dictionary. Divide it into syllables. Write **SC** if there is a sentence clue in the dictionary. Write **PC** if there is a picture clue.

1. *apple*   *ap·ple* _____

2. _____   _____   _____

3. _____   _____   _____

4. _____   _____   _____

5. _____   _____   _____

6. _____   _____   _____

7. _____   _____   _____

Writing

Write a sentence with each group of spelling words. You may add the endings **s, ed, ing, y, er,** and **est**. Remember that all your spelling words end with a silent **e**!

1. nibble, apple, cattle

_____

- -

_____

- -

_____

2. bubble, puddle, middle

_____

- -

_____

- -

_____

3. bottle, juggle, giggle

_____

- -

_____

- -

_____

4. little, wiggle, rattle

_____

- -

_____

- -

_____

Reach Out for New Words

A Words are printed in three directions in this puzzle. → ↓ ↘ Find and circle each new word. Then write the words.

s	d	r	i	b	b	l	e
e	a	t	c	a	b	r	f
t	q	d	u	t	c	s	i
t	d	b	d	t	n	p	d
l	g	f	d	l	w	v	d
e	l	k	l	e	e	m	l
h	j	k	e	t	t	l	e
h	u	d	d	l	e	x	z

1. _____
2. _____
3. _____
4. _____
5. _____
6. _____
7. _____
8. _____

B Find the word in each sentence that does not make sense. Replace that word with a new word that rhymes with it.

_____

1. Terry plays the riddle. _____

2. Help me put the paddle on my horse. _____

3. Scribble the basketball down the court. _____

4. Our toy soldiers fought a cattle. _____

5. I love to muddle the baby! _____

6. The football players met in a puddle. _____

air	+	plane	=	airplane	*airplane*
air	+	port	=	airport	*airport*
out	+	side	=	outside	*outside*
in	+	side	=	inside	*inside*
up	+	stairs	=	upstairs	*upstairs*
bed	+	room	=	bedroom	*bedroom*
class	+	room	=	classroom	*classroom*
after	+	noon	=	afternoon	*afternoon*
week	+	end	=	weekend	*weekend*
some	+	times	=	sometimes	*sometimes*
an	+	other	=	another	*another*
any	+	thing	=	anything	*anything*
may	+	be	=	maybe	*maybe*
break	+	fast	=	breakfast	*breakfast*
out	+	fit	=	outfit	*outfit*

1. The words in the last column are **compound words**.
   Each compound word is made from how many smaller words? ____
2. Did the spellings of the smaller words
   change when they were put together? ____

> A **compound word** is made from two smaller words.
> Do not change the spellings of the words when you put them together.

A Write the spelling words that complete the story.

My friend Tommy once flew on a jet _____ .

Now he loves planes. At school I _____ see him

staring out the window of our _____ . He is watching

the planes land at the nearby _____ .

Last _____ Tommy's parents took us to the

airport. First we went to the snack shop _____ the

terminal building. We ate _____ . Then we went

_____ and climbed _____ to

the observation deck. We watched one jet after another take off or land.

Since Tommy loves planes so much, _____ he

will become a pilot! I can't think of anything he'd like better!

Proofreading

B Cross out the misspelled words. Write the words correctly.

1. *Do you have enough money to buy anuther outfit?*

2. *The areplane lands late this aftrenoon.*

3. *Take your costume upstares to your bedroome.*

C Use each clue to find a spelling word that fits in the puzzle.

1. perhaps

2. a place to sleep

3. once in a while

4. where students learn

5. Saturday and Sunday

6. clothes you wear

7. something

8. opposite of **outside**

9. opposite of **inside**

What word do you see in the colored boxes? _____

178

airplane	inside	classroom	sometimes	maybe
airport	upstairs	afternoon	another	breakfast
outside	bedroom	weekend	anything	outfit

Build Word Power

Look at the first pair of words in each row. Write a word from the box that makes the second pair of words go together in the same way as the first pair.

1. **drive** is to **car**   as **fly** is to

2. **train** is to **station**   as **airplane** is to

3. **bottom** is to **top**   as **downstairs** is to

4. **cook** is to **kitchen**   as **sleep** is to

5. **seat** is to **bus**   as **desk** is to

6. **A.M.** is to **morning**   as **P.M.** is to

7. **Monday** is to **weekday**   as **Sunday** is to

8. **grass** is to **outside**   as **carpet** is to

Search for new words!
Follow the directions below.

Reach Out for New Words

A Rematch the word parts of these silly compounds to make real compound words. Change only the underlined parts. Use each word part once. Cross out each underlined word as you use it.

1. some<u>light</u>

2. basket<u>paper</u>

3. them<u>ground</u>

4. book<u>walk</u>

5. flash<u>fish</u>

6. rain<u>selves</u>

7. gold<u>ball</u>

8. side<u>mark</u>

9. play<u>one</u>

10. news<u>coat</u>

B Write the new word that might be found in each place.

1. in a bowl of water

2. between some pages

3. going through a net

4. in a dark room

5. out in a storm

6. next to the street

28. wrapper know climb

29. fair unfair / tie untie / lock unlock

30. paint repaint / pay repay / turn return

31. let us let's / do not don't / he will he'll

32. mother mother's / father father's / baby baby's

33. apple puzzle nibble

34. upstairs bedroom afternoon

Using Review Words

A Look at the first pair of words in each row. Write a spelling word that makes the second pair of words go together in the same way.

1. **paint** is to **repaint**   as   **pay** is to   _____

2. **noon** is to **afternoon**   as   **room** is to   _____

3. **let us** is to **let's**   as   **do not** is to   _____

4. **untie** is to **tie**   as   **unlock** is to   _____

5. **mother** is to **mother's**   as   **father** is to   _____

6. **room** is to **bedroom**   as   **stairs** is to   _____

7. **don't** is to **do not**   as   **he'll** is to   _____

8. **tie** is to **untie**   as   **fair** is to   _____

9. **father's** is to **father**   as   **baby's** is to   _____

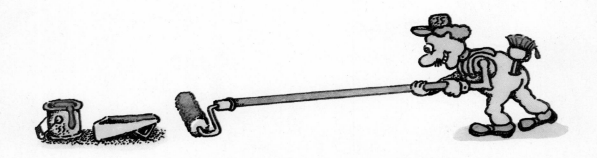

Proofreading

B Cross out the spelling mistakes. Then write each misspelled word correctly.

1. Let's reppaint our kitchen chairs this aftrenoon.

_____   _____

_ _ _ _ _ _ _ _ _ _ _ _ _ _   _ _ _ _ _ _ _ _ _ _ _ _ _ _

_____   _____

2. This key will unlock my mothers suitcase.

_____

_ _ _ _ _ _ _ _ _ _ _ _ _ _

_____

3. My pony likes to nible on a piece of appel.

_____   _____

_ _ _ _ _ _ _ _ _ _ _ _ _ _   _ _ _ _ _ _ _ _ _ _ _ _ _ _

_____   _____

4. He'l retturn my watch tomorrow.

_____   _____

_ _ _ _ _ _ _ _ _ _ _ _ _ _   _ _ _ _ _ _ _ _ _ _ _ _ _ _

_____   _____

C Complete each phrase with a word from the box.

| puzzle | baby's | wrapper | climb |
| let's | know | untie | unlock |

1. _____ the door

2. a candy _____

3. a crossword _____

4. _____ a ladder

5. _____ go out

6. _____ rattle

7. _____ the knot

8. _____ his name

183

Using More Review Words

A Use the directions following each base word to make another form of the word.

1. **write**   add prefix meaning **again**

2. **how**   form contraction using **is**

3. **kind**   add prefix meaning **not**

4. **true**   add prefix meaning **not**

5. **you**   form contraction using **have**

6. **opened** add prefix meaning **not**

7. **man**   show possessive form

8. **that**   form contraction using **is**

9. **we**   form contraction using **will**

10. **girl**   show possessive form

11. **visit**   add prefix meaning **again**

12. **sister**   show possessive form

13. **willing** add prefix meaning **not**

14. **uncle**   show possessive form

15. **we**   form contraction using **are**

B Three words in each row follow the same spelling pattern. One word does not. Find that word. Be ready to tell why it does not belong.

1. comb   sometimes   inside   another

2. outside   unpack   unplug   unbutton

3. knuckle   knee   knew   wreck

4. wasn't   aunt's   didn't   aren't

5. uncover   reread   lamb   uneven

6. who's   boy's   woman's   brother's

7. wrong   weekend   knee   crumb

C Look at the first pair of words. Write a word from the box that makes the second pair of words go together in the same way.

> *middle   wrist   wrong   little*
> *unwrap   knee   unbutton*

1. **shoe** is to **untie**   as   **shirt** is to   _____

2. **elephant** is to **big**   as   **mouse** is to   _____

3. **foot** is to **ankle**   as   **hand** is to   _____

4. **head** is to **top**   as   **waist** is to   _____

5. **spell** is to **misspell** as   **right** is to   _____

6. **arm** is to **elbow**   as   **leg** is to   _____

7. **banana** is to **peel**   as   **gift** is to   _____

185

twins	pair	closet	suitcase
fixed	gloves	trunk	stacked
hair	jacket	morning	woolen
worn	dresser	overslept	bedspread

Prewriting. Prewriting is thinking of ideas for a story. Writers plan their stories before they begin to write.

Use Prewriting Skills

Use the spelling words to write a story about twins going on a trip.

1. What two things can be worn? _____   _____

2. What are four places to put clothes?

   _____   _____

   _____   _____

3. Which four words tell about actions that happened in the past?

   _____   _____

   _____   _____

4. Which three compound words might you use in your story?

   _____   _____   _____

Now Think Think about twins getting ready to go on a trip. How old are they? Do they look alike or are they different? Are they going away for a weekend or for a long vacation? Think about the clothes they must pack. On your own paper, write some of your ideas for a story.

Writing. The people in a story are called **characters.** Writers must choose words that make the characters and the setting seem real.

Use Writing Skills

A Make each word group below into a good topic sentence. Each sentence should tell about twins who are going on a trip.

1. For weeks, Jerry and Jill ____ .

2. Today was finally the day when ____ .

Use good describing words to make a story seem real. Describing words paint a picture in your reader's mind.

Example: The bird was very strange. It had a tiny head and a huge beak. It had no neck at all. The body was round with short wings. Its long, thin legs were like stilts.

B Look at the describing words in each word group below. Then use each group in a complete sentence.

1. pair of warm, furry gloves

2. curly black hair

3. bright sunny morning

4. stuffed into the small suitcase

5. red woolen jacket

6. tall thin twins

Now Write   Write a first draft of your story.

1. Begin with a topic sentence. Do you want to use one of the sentences from Exercise A?

2. Try to use some of the sentences you wrote for Exercise B.

3. Use words that describe the characters and setting of your story.

Revising. Revising means changing parts of a first draft to make it better. First, revise your ideas. Then proofread for mistakes.

Use Revising and Proofreading Skills

A Revise this story. Then copy the revised story on your paper.

1. Find and correct two incomplete sentences.

2. Find two sentences with missing words. Find one sentence with two extra words.

3. Cross out a sentence that doesn't fit the main idea.

Summertime had finally arrived. The Henley twins were almost ready for vacation. Leaving for the airport. The few things left to pack were stacked beside open suitcase.

"Nothing else will fit," groaned Shannon.

"No wonder," laughed Sharon. "There's nothing left in our closet! It looks as if we're going away for two years, not two months." She put two red woolen jackets back in the closet. Some other things in the dresser drawer.

Shannon said, "Leave our warm, furry gloves packed," Shannon said. "Canada is supposed to be cold." Canada is the second largest country in the world. Sharon snapped the suitcase closed.

"Wait!" Shannon yelled. "Where's the cat? She was sitting on the bedspread a minute ago." The twins looked at each other and started to laugh. Shannon opened the suitcase again. A frightened, furry white cat out onto the bed.

B Practice your proofreading skills on the story below. Correct the six misspelled words. Circle and correct six punctuation errors and four capitalization errors.

Remember
- Days of the week and proper names are capitalized.
- A period should not separate parts of one thought.
- A comma is used after each word in a series.
- An apostrophe is used in contractions.
- Quotation marks are used at the beginning and end of a speaker's words.

Tim and kim were going camping for the weekend. Kim was

awake at five oclock Saturday morning. She had stacked

everything she needed. On top of the dressar friday night. Now

she packed in a hurry. Then she woke Tim, who always

oversleped.

"Come on, sleepyhead," she said. Mom has fixt Breakfast

for us already."

Tim kicked off his bedspred and jumped to his feet. He put on

his jeans a jackett and an old pair of sneakers. He grabbed

some clothes out of the closit and rolled them in his sleeping

bag. Then he raced downstairs before Kim had finished eating.

"Come on, slowpoke, he said. "Do you want to make us late?"

1. _____   4. _____

2. _____   5. _____

3. _____   6. _____

Now Revise Read the first draft of your story. Are all the sentences complete?
Did you use good describing words?
Proofread and correct mistakes in capitalization, punctuation, and
spelling. Write the final copy of your story in your best handwriting.

Handbook

I. The Structure of Words

Syllables
Base Words
Prefixes
Word Endings
Contractions
Compound Words

II. The Function of Words

Nouns
Singular Nouns
Plural Nouns
Possessive Form of Nouns
Possessive Pronouns
Verbs
Past Tense Verbs
Adjectives

III. The Sound of Words

Vowels
Long Vowels
Short Vowels
Consonants
Silent Letters

I. **The Structure of Words** means the way words are put together.

Syllables

Words are made up of parts called syllables. The dictionary shows how words are divided into syllables.

but·ter = two syllables
dress = one syllable

Base Words

Base words are words before any changes have been made.

Base word	wrap
Base word with endings added	wraps
	wrapped
	wrapping
Base word with prefix added	unwrap

Prefixes

A prefix is a syllable added to the beginning of a word to change the meaning.

I wrapped the birthday present.
(I put the paper on the present.)

I unwrapped the birthday present.
(I took the paper off the present.)

I rewrapped the birthday present.
(I put the paper back on the present.)

Word Endings

Word endings are letters added to the end of a word to change the way it is used.

play	Ryan will play ball.	(verb)
plays	Ryan plays ball.	(verb)
playing	Ryan is playing ball.	(verb)
played	Ryan played ball yesterday.	(past tense verb)
player	Ryan is a good player.	(noun)

Contractions

A contraction is made from two words. When the two words are put together, an apostrophe takes the place of one or more letters.

we are =	we **a**re	=	we're
he will =	he **wi**ll	=	he'll

Compound Words

A compound word is made from two smaller words. The spellings do not change when the words are put together.

class + room = classroom
after + noon = afternoon

Nouns

A noun is a word that names something.

The <u>monkey</u> ate a <u>banana</u>.

The sentence has two words that are nouns.

Singular Nouns

A noun that names one thing is called a singular noun. The two nouns in this sentence are singular:

The <u>monkey</u> ate a <u>banana</u>.
(one monkey)   (one banana)

Plural Nouns

A noun that names more than one thing is a plural noun.

The <u>monkeys</u> ate a banana.
(more than one monkey)

The monkey ate two <u>bananas</u>.
(more than one banana)

Possessive Form of Nouns

The possessive form of a noun shows that something belongs to someone. Make the possessive form of a noun by adding **'s**.

That car belongs to my father.
That is my <u>father's</u> car.

Possessive Pronouns

A possessive pronoun takes the place of a noun in the
possessive form.

> My father's car = his car
> The Clark's house = their house
> Ashley's book = her book

A possessive pronoun is not spelled with an apostrophe.

Verbs

A verb is a word that tells about an action.

> I walk on the beach in the summertime.
> (Walk tells what I do.)

Past Tense Verbs

A verb that tells about an action that happened in the past is in
the past tense.

> We walked a mile to the beach.
> We ran along the edge of the water.
> (Walked and ran tell what we did.)

Adjectives

An adjective is a word that describes something.

> We walked on the sandy beach.
> (Sandy describes the beach.)

> We ran into the cold water.
> (Cold describes the water.)

III. The Sound of Words means the way you say words when you speak. Sometimes the sound will help you to spell a word.

Vowels

Five letters of the alphabet are called vowels. The vowels are **a**, **e**, **i**, **o**, and **u**.

Long Vowels

Long vowels are easy to hear because they "say their own names."

a	**e**	**i**	**o**	**u**
nation	me	fine	no	unit

Short Vowels

Short vowels sound like the vowels in these words:

a	**e**	**i**	**o**	**u**
at	ten	is	lot	up

Consonants

The consonants are all the letters of the alphabet except **a**, **e**, **i**, **o**, and **u**.

Silent Letters

Silent letters make no sound. You can see them in a word, but you cannot hear them.

Many words have a final silent **e**.

The last letter you see in the word hope is e.
The last letter you hear in the word hope is p.

Many words begin with a silent **k** or **w**.

The first letter you see in the word k<u>n</u>ee is k.
The first letter you hear in the word kn<u>e</u>e is n.

The first letter you see in the word <u>w</u>rist is w.
The first letter you hear in the word <u>wri</u>st is r.

Some words end with a silent **b**.

clim<u>b</u>   com<u>b</u>   lam<u>b</u>

Two letters are silent in the combination **igh**.
The letters **g** and **h** make no sound.

ri<u>gh</u>t   hi<u>gh</u>   li<u>gh</u>t

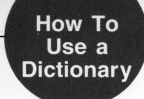

How To Use a Dictionary

How To Find a Word

A dictionary is organized like a telephone book. It lists information in alphabetical order with guide words at the top of each page.

Guide Words

The guide words help you find the right page quickly. They tell you at a glance what section of the alphabet is included on each page. The guide word on the left tells you the first word on that page. The guide word on the right tells you the last word on that page. If the word you are looking for comes alphabetically between those two words, you are on the right page.

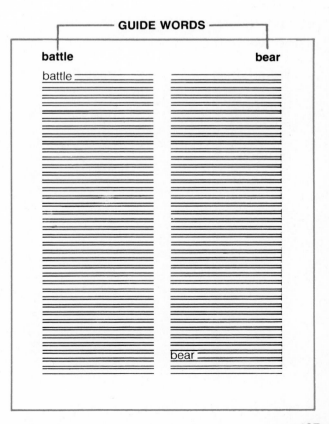

Alphabetical Order

Alphabetical order means the order of the letters in the alphabet.

Words beginning with **a** come first.   **a**bout
Words beginning with **b** come next.   **b**ear
Words beginning with **c** come   **c**lass
   after words beginning with **b**.

When two words begin with the same letter, you must look at the second letter of each word to determine alphabetical order. When several of the letters are the same, you will have to look at the third or fourth letter to determine the alphabetical order.

toa**d**   The first three letters in the words <u>toad</u> and <u>toast</u>
toa**st**   are the same. The fourth letter must be used to determine alphabetical order. Since **d** comes before **s**, <u>toad</u> is alphabetized before <u>toast</u>.

Words Listed

The words listed in a dictionary are called entry words. A word is usually listed in its base form. Other forms of the word may be listed within the same entry.

Word Forms	Base Form	Entry Word
hurrying hurried	hurry	hurry
dances dancing	dance	dance

What the Dictionary Tells About a Word

A dictionary tells you much more than the spelling and meaning of a word. The information it contains about each word is called the *entry*. The parts of an entry are labeled and explained below.

The ENTRY WORD is printed in heavy black type. It is divided into syllables.

A PICTURE may be used to help you understand the meaning of the entry word.

The PART OF SPEECH is shown after the pronunciation.

The RESPELLING tells you how to pronounce the word. The *Pronunciation Key* explains the respelling.

A STRESS MARK is placed after a syllable that gets an accent.

The DEFINITION is the meaning of the word. If a word has more than one meaning, each meaning is given a number.

OTHER FORMS of the entry word are included in the same entry.

A sample SENTENCE; can help you understand the meaning of the entry word.

mouse (mous) *noun*   a small, gnawing animal. —*plural* **mice**

mouth (mouth) *noun*   the opening in the head for eating and making sounds [The soup burned my *mouth*.] —*plural* **mouths**

move (mo̅o̅v) *verb*   **1** to change place or position [*Move* the picture to the left.] **2** to change the place where one lives [They *moved* to New York.] —**moved, mov′ ing**

mud·dy (mud′ ē) *adjective*   full of mud [Clean your *muddy* boots.] —**mud′ di·er, mud′ di·est**

mul·ti·ply (mul′ tə plī) *verb*   to repeat a figure a certain number of times [She *multiplied* 3 by 4 to get 12.] —**mul′ ti·plied, mul′ ti·ply·ing**

N

nap·kin (nap′ kin) *noun*   a piece of cloth or paper used while eating to protect clothes or to wipe fingers or lips. —*plural* **nap′ kins**

near (nir) *adjective*   not far; close [Our house is *near* to the school.] —**near′ er, near′ est**

neigh·bor (nā′ bər) *noun*   a person who lives near another. —*plural* **neigh′ bors**

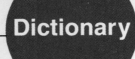

Dictionary

Pronunciation Key

SYMBOL	KEY WORDS	SYMBOL	KEY WORDS	SYMBOL	KEY WORDS
a	ask, fat	u	up, cut	n	not, ton
ā	ape, date	ur	fur, fern	p	put, tap
ä	car, lot			r	red, dear
		ə	a in ago	s	sell, pass
e	elf, ten		e in agent	t	top, hat
er	berry, care		e in father	v	vat, have
ē	even, meet		i in unity	w	will, always
			o in collect	y	yet, yard
i	is, hit		u in focus	z	zebra, haze
ir	mirror, here				
ī	ice, fire			ch	chin, arch
		b	bed, dub	ng	ring, singer
ō	open, go	d	did, had	sh	she, dash
ô	law, horn	f	fall, off	th	thin, truth
oi	oil, point	g	get, dog	*th*	then, father
oo	look, pull	h	he, ahead	zh	s in pleasure
o͞o	ooze, tool	j	joy, jump		
yoo	unite, cure	k	kill, bake	'	as in (ā'b'l)
yoo	cute, few	l	let, ball		
ou	out, crowd	m	met, trim		

A heavy stress mark ' is placed after a syllable that gets a strong accent, as in **con·sid·er** (kən sid'ər).

A light stress mark ' is placed after a syllable that also gets an accent, but of a weaker kind, as in **dic·tion·ar·y** (dik'shən er'ē).

The dictionary definitions used throughout this book were specially prepared by the staff of McDougal, Littell & Company and are based upon the entries in *Webster's New World Dictionary for Young Readers* with the consent of the publisher of that work, Simon & Schuster, Inc.

A

a·ble (ā′ b'l) *adjective* having the power to do something [She is *able* to take care of herself.] —**a′ bler, a′ blest**

a·bout (ə bout′) *preposition* having to do with [This is a book *about* ships.]

a·corn (ā′ kôrn) *noun* the nut of the oak tree. —*plural* **a′ corns**

a·cross (ə krôs′) *preposition* from one side to the other [We swam *across* the river.]

ad·dress (ə dres′ *or* ad′ res) *noun* the place where mail is sent. —*plural* **ad′ dress·es**

a·fraid (ə frād′) *adjective* feeling fear [I'm *afraid* of the dark.]

af·ter·noon (af tər noon′) *noun* the time of day from noon to evening. —*plural* **af·ter·noons′**

air·plane (er′ plān) *noun* an aircraft driven forward by a jet engine or propeller. —*plural* **air′ planes**

air·port (er′ pôrt) *noun* a place where aircraft take off and land. —*plural* **air′ ports**

all (ôl) *adjective* the whole thing or amount [I have *all* the gold.]

al·ley (al′ ē) *noun* a narrow street behind buildings [The garbage truck drove down the *alley*.] —*plural* **al′ leys**

al·most (ôl′ mōst) *adverb* not completely; very nearly [He tripped and *almost* fell.]

al·so (ôl′ sō) *adverb* in addition; too; besides [The man who directed the show *also* acted in it.]

al·ways (ôl′ wiz *or* ôl′ wāz) *adverb* at all times [*Always* be courteous.]

A·mer·i·ca (ə mer′ ə kə) *noun* North America or South America.

a·mount (ə mount′) *noun* total [The bill was $50, but he paid only half that *amount*.]

an·oth·er (ə nu*th*′ ər) *adjective* **1** one more [Take *another* apple.] **2** a different one [Exchange the book for *another* one.]

ant (ant) *noun* a small insect that lives in or on the ground [Many *ants* crawled near our picnic.] —*plural* **ants**

an·y·thing (en′ ē thing) *pronoun* any object, event, or fact [Did *anything* important happen today?]

ap·pear (ə pir′) *verb* to come into sight [A ship *appeared* on the horizon.] —**ap·peared′, ap·pear′ ing**

ap·ple (ap′ 'l) *noun* a round, firm fruit with green, yellow, or red skin. —*plural* **ap′ ples**

are·n't (ärnt) are not [They *aren't* going.]

ar·gue (är′ gyoo) *verb* quarrel [The children were *arguing* about whose turn it was.] —**ar′ gued, ar′ gu·ing**

ar·my (är′ mē) *noun* a large group of soldiers. —*plural* **ar′ mies**

a·round (ə round′) *adverb* in a circle [The wheel turned *around*.]

ar·row (ar′ ō) *noun* a thin rod that is shot from a bow. —*plural* **ar′ rows**

ash (ash) *noun* the powder left after something has burned. —*plural* **ash′ es**

ask (ask) *verb* to use words in trying to find out [We *asked* how much it cost.] —**asked, ask′ ing**

a	fat	ir	here	ou	out	zh	leisure
ā	ape	ī	bite, fire	u	up	ng	ring
ä	car, lot	ō	go	ʉr	fur		a *in* ago
e	ten	ô	law, horn	ch	chin		e *in* agent
er	care	oi	oil	sh	she	ə =	i *in* unity
ē	even	oo	look	th	thin		o *in* collect
i	hit	oo	tool	*th*	then		u *in* focus

at·tic (at′ ik) *noun*   the space just below the roof of a house. —*plural* **at′ tics**

aunt (ant or änt) *noun*   a sister of one's mother or father. —*plural* **aunts**

aw·ful (ô′ fəl) *adjective*   very bad, terrible: *used only in everyday talk* [The weather was *awful*.]

ax (aks) *noun*   a tool for chopping wood [Lincoln split logs with an *ax*.] —*plural* **ax′ es**

B

ba·by (bā′ bē) *noun*   infant. —*plural* **ba′ bies**

bag·gy (bag′ ē) *adjective*   hanging loosely [The pants were *baggy* at the knees.] —**bag′ gi·er, bag′ gi·est**

bak·er (bāk′ ər) *noun*   a person whose work is baking bread, cakes, and pastry. —*plural* **bak′ ers**

bak·er·y (bāk′ ər ē) *noun*   a place where bread and cakes are baked or sold. —*plural* **bak′ er·ies**

ba·nan·a (bə nan′ ə) *noun*   a large yellow fruit [Mother brought a bunch of *bananas*.] —*plural* **ba·nan′as**

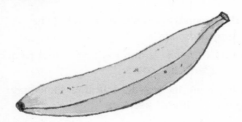

bas·ket (bas′ kit) *noun*   a container, often with handles [The apples were placed in a *basket*.] —*plural* **bas′ kets**

bas·ket·ball (bas′ kit bôl) *noun*   a game played by two teams of five players.

bat·tle (bat′ ′l) *noun*   warfare [He limps from a wound received in *battle*.] —*plural* **bat′ tles**

bay (bā) *noun*   a part of a sea or lake that forms a curve in the coastline [The boat sailed across the *bay*.] —*plural* **bays**

bear (ber) *noun*   a large, heavy animal with fur and a short tail. —*plural* **bears**

beard (bird) *noun*   the hair growing on the lower part of a man's face. —*plural* **beards**

beau·ti·ful (byo͞ot′ ə fəl) *adjective*   very pleasant to look at or hear [She has a *beautiful* face.]

bed (bed) *noun*   furniture to sleep or rest on. —*plural* **beds**

bed·room (bed′ ro͞om) *noun*   a room with a bed, for sleeping in. —*plural* **bed′ rooms**

bed·spread (bed′ spred) *noun*   a cover spread over a bed when it is not being slept in. —*plural* **bed′ spreads**

bee (bē) *noun*   an insect that has four wings and feeds on the nectar of flowers. —*plural* **bees**

beg (beg) *verb*   to ask as a favor [She *begged* us not to tell the secret.] —**begged, beg′ ging**

ber·ry (ber′ ē) *noun*   any small, juicy fruit with seeds. —*plural* **ber′ ries**

big (big) *adjective*   large [That's a *big* dog.] —**big′ ger, big′ gest**

birth·day (burth′ dā) *noun*   the day on which a person is born. —*plural* **birth′ days**

blan·ket (blang′ kit) *noun*   a large cover to sit on or lie under [A picnic lunch was spread on the *blanket*.] —*plural* **blan′ kets**

blouse (blous) *noun*   a garment like a shirt. —*plural* **blous′ es**

blue·jay (blo͞o′ jā) *noun*   a bird with a blue back and feathers. —*plural* **blue′ jays**

boast (bōst) *verb*   to brag or talk about with too much pride [He *boasted* about his bravery.] —**boast′ ed, boast′ ing**

boat (bōt) *noun*   a small vessel used for traveling on water. —*plural* **boats**

bod·y (bäd′ ē) *noun*   all parts of a person or animal. —*plural* **bod′ ies**

book·mark (book′ märk) *noun*   something that marks a place in a book. —*plural* **book′ marks**

bore (bôr) *verb*   to make tired by being dull [The speaker *bored* the crowd.] —**bored, bor′ ing**

born (bôrn) *a past form of* **bear** given birth to [The twins were *born* an hour apart.]

both·er (bäth′ ər) *verb* to annoy [Does the noise *bother* you?] —**both′ ered, both′ er·ing**

bot·tle (bät′ ′l) *noun* a container usually made of glass or plastic [Get the *bottle* of milk.] —*plural* **bot′ tles**

bounce (bouns) *verb* to hit against a surface so as to spring back [They *bounced* the ball against the wall.] —**bounced, bounc′ ing**

bound (bound) *verb* to move with a leap or leaps [The dog came *bounding* to meet her.] —**bound′ ed, bound′ ing**

box (bäks) *noun* a container used to hold or carry things in. —*plural* **box′ es**

boy (boi) *noun* a male child. —*plural* **boys**

brag (brag) *verb* to boast [She *bragged* about winning the race.] —**bragged, brag′ ging**

brave (brāv) *adjective* full of courage; not afraid. —**brav′ er, brav′ est**

break·fast (brek′ fəst) *noun* the first meal of the day.

breeze (brēz) *noun* a light wind. —*plural* **breez′ es**

bright (brīt) *adjective* **1** full of light [Some stars are very *bright*.] **2** clever [My brother is a *bright* child.] —**bright′ er, bright′ est**

bro·ken (brō′ kən) *adjective* split into pieces [Pick up the *broken* dish.]

broth·er (bru*th*′ ər) *noun* a boy or man as he is related to the other children of his parents. —*plural* **broth′ ers**

brush (brush) *noun* a bunch of bristles fastened together for cleaning, painting, or grooming. —*plural* **brush′ es** ◆*verb* to use a brush to clean, paint, or groom [*Brush* your teeth well.] —**brushed, brush′ ing**

bub·ble (bub′ ′l) *noun* a thin film of liquid forming a ball around air [Look at the soap *bubbles*.] —*plural* **bub′ bles**

build (bild) *verb* to make by putting together parts [Let's *build* a house.] —**built, build′ ing**

bun·ny (bun′ ē) *noun* a rabbit. —*plural* **bun′ nies**

burn (bʉrn) *verb* to be on fire [The candle *burned* brightly.] —**burned, burn′ ing**

burst (bʉrst) *verb* to break open suddenly; explode [The balloon *burst* with a loud pop.] — **burst, burst′ ing**

bur·y (ber′ ē) *verb* to put something under the ground [The dog *buried* its bone.] —**bur′ ied, bur′ y·ing**

bus (bus) *noun* a large motor coach that carries passengers. —*plural* **bus′ es**

but·ter (but′ ər) *noun* a spread for bread or cooking made by churning cream.

but·ter·fly (but′ ər flī) *noun* an insect with four colorful wings. —*plural* **but′ ter·flies**

buy (bī) *verb* to get by paying money [The Dutch *bought* Manhattan Island for about $24.] —**bought, buy′ ing**

C

cab·bage (kab′ ij) *noun* a vegetable with thick leaves folded tightly to form a head [*Cabbage* may be eaten cooked or raw.] —*plural* **cab′ bag·es**

cage (kāj) *noun* a closed-off space with wires or bars on the sides, in which to keep birds or animals. —*plural* **cag′ es**

a	fat	ir	here	ou	out	zh	leisure
ā	ape	ī	bite, fire	u	up	ng	ring
ä	car, lot	ō	go	ʉr	fur		a *in* ago
e	ten	ô	law, horn	ch	chin		e *in* agent
er	care	oi	oil	sh	she	ə =	i *in* unity
ē	even	oo	look	th	thin		o *in* collect
i	hit	o͞o	tool	*th*	then		u *in* focus

calf (kaf) *noun* a young cow or bull. —*plural* **calves**

can·dy (kan′ dē) *noun* a sweet food made from sugar or syrup. —*plural* **can′ dies**

car·ri·er (kar′ ē ər) *noun* a person or thing that carries [A mail *carrier* delivered the package.] —*plural* **car′ ri·ers**

car·rot (kar′ ət) *noun* a plant with a long, orange root eaten as a vegetable. —*plural* **car′ rots**

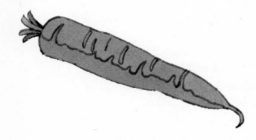

car·ry (kar′ ē) *verb* to take from one place to another [Please help me *carry* these books upstairs.] —**car′ ried, car′ ry·ing**

catch (kach) *verb* **1** to take hold of a person or thing that is moving [to *catch* a thief]. **2** to stop with the hands [to *catch* a ball]. —**caught, catch′ ing**

catch·er (kach′ ər) *noun* in baseball, one who catches pitched balls not hit by the batter. —*plural* **catch′ ers**

cat·tle (kat′ ′l) *plural noun* animals of the cow family raised on farms and ranches.

change (chānj) *verb* to make or become different [She *changed* her mind.] —**changed, chang′ ing**

char·coal (chär′ kōl) *noun* a form of carbon used as a fuel or filter.

chase (chās) *verb* to follow in order to catch. —**chased, chas′ ing**

cher·ry (cher′ ē) *noun* a small, round, red fruit. —*plural* **cher′ ries**

chess (ches) *noun* a game played on a chessboard by two players.

child (chīld) *noun* a young boy or girl. —*plural* **chil′ dren**

chill (chil) *noun* a feeling of coldness [There was a *chill* in the air.] —*plural* **chills**

chim·ney (chim′ nē) *noun* a pipe or shaft that carries off smoke. —*plural* **chim′ neys**

chop (chäp) *verb* to cut with an ax or other sharp tool [The lumberjack *chopped* down a tree.] —**chopped, chop′ ping**

cit·y (sit′ ē) *noun* a large town. —*plural* **cit′ ies**

clap (klap) *verb* to hit the palms of the hands together [The audience *clapped* after the play.] —**clapped, clap′ ping**

class (klas) *noun* a group of students meeting together to be taught [My English *class* is at 9 o'clock.] —*plural* **class′ es**

class·room (klas′ rōōm) *noun* a room in a school where classes meet to be taught. —*plural* **class′ rooms**

clean (klēn) *adjective* without dirt [The room is *clean*.] —**clean′ er, clean′ est** ◆*verb* to remove dirt from [Please *clean* the oven.] —**cleaned, clean′ ing**

clear (klir) *adjective* without clouds [Today was a *clear*, sunny day.] —**clear′ er, clear′ est**

cliff (klif) *noun* a steep rock that goes almost straight down. —*plural* **cliffs**

climb (klīm) *verb* to go up or down using feet or hands [We like to *climb* up trees.] —**climbed, climb′ ing**

clock (kläk) *noun* a device for measuring and showing time. —*plural* **clocks**

close (klōz) *verb* to shut [*Close* the door.] —**closed, clos′ ing**

clos·et (kläz′ it) *noun* a small room or cupboard for clothes, linens, or supplies [The clothes were hung in the *closet*.] —*plural* **clos′ ets**

cloud (kloud) *noun* many drops of water floating in the air. —*plural* **clouds**

coach (kōch) *noun* a person who teaches and trains athletes or students. —*plural* **coach′ es**

coast (kōst) *noun*　land along the sea [The boat sailed toward the *coast*.] —*plural* **coasts**

coat (kōt) *noun*　an outer garment with sleeves. —*plural* **coats**

co·coa (kō′ kō) *noun*　a drink made from the powder of roasted cacao seeds.

colt (kōlt) *noun*　a young male horse or donkey [The *colt* stood by its mother.] —*plural* **colts**

comb (kōm) *noun*　a thin strip of hard material with teeth, used to arrange hair. ◆*verb*　to smooth or clean with a comb. —**combed, comb′ ing**

come (kum) *verb*　to move from there to here [Will you *come* to our party?] —**came, come, com′ ing**

com·pa·ny (kum′ pə nē) *noun*　**1** a group of people joined in some work [She works for a large *company*.] **2** guest or guests [We invited *company* for dinner.] —*plural* **com′ pa·nies**

com·pass (kum′ pəs) *noun*　an instrument for showing direction. —*plural* **com′ pass·es**

cop·i·er (käp′ ē ər) *noun*　a duplicating machine. —*plural* **cop′ i·ers**

cop·y (käp′ ē) *noun*　imitation [Make four *copies* of this letter.] —*plural* **cop′ ies** ◆*verb*　to make a copy or copies of [*Copy* the questions on the chalkboard.] —**cop′ ied, cop′ y·ing**

corn (kôrn) *noun*　a grain that grows in kernels on large ears.

cor·ner (kôr′ nər) *noun*　the place where two streets meet. —*plural* **cor′ ners**

cot·ton (kät′ ′n) *noun*　a type of cloth [This shirt is made of *cotton*.] —*plural* **cot′ tons**

couch (kouch) *noun*　furniture for sitting on; sofa. —*plural* **couch′ es**

could·n't (kood′ ′nt) could not.

count (kount) *verb*　to name numbers in order [Can you *count* to fifty?] —**count′ ed, count′ ing**

cous·in (kuz′ ′n) *noun*　the son or daughter of one's uncle or aunt. —*plural* **cous′ ins**

cow·boy (kou′ boi) *noun*　a ranch worker who herds cattle. —*plural* **cow′ boys**

crack·er (krak′ ər) *noun*　a thin, crisp biscuit. —*plural* **crack′ ers**

crash (krash) *verb*　to hit with great force [The bull *crashed* through the fence.] —**crashed, crash′ ing** ◆*noun*　the smashing of a car or airplane [They were hurt in a car *crash*.] —*plural* **crash′ es**

creek (krēk *or* krik) *noun*　a small stream [A *creek* wound through the meadow.] —*plural* **creeks**

crumb (krum) *noun*　a tiny piece broken off from bread or cake. —*plural* **crumbs**

crunch (krunch) *verb*　to chew with a noisy, crackling sound [*Crunch* the raw carrots.] —**crunch′ es, crunch′ ing**

crunch·y (krunch′ ē) *adjective*　making a crunching sound. —**crunch′ i·er, crunch′ i·est**

cry (krī) *verb*　to show feeling by shedding tears. —**cried, cry′ ing**

cud·dle (kud′ ′l) *verb*　to hold lovingly in one's arms [I like to *cuddle* the baby.] —**cud′ dled, cud′ dling**

a fat	**ir** here	**ou** out	**zh** leisure
ā ape	**ī** bite, fire	**u** up	**ng** ring
ä car, lot	**ō** go	**ʉr** fur	a *in* ago
e ten	**ô** law, horn	**ch** chin	e *in* agent
er care	**oi** oil	**sh** she	ə = i *in* unity
ē even	**oo** look	**th** thin	o *in* collect
i hit	**ōo** tool	**th** then	u *in* focus

D

dai·sy (dā′ zē) *noun*   a common flower with white or pink petals around a yellow center. —*plural* **dai′ sies**

danc·er (dan′ sər) *noun*   a person who dances. —*plural* **danc′ ers**

dark (därk) *adjective*   having little or no light [This is a *dark* room.] —**dark′ er, dark′ est**

daugh·ter (dôt′ ər) *noun*   a girl or woman as she is related to a parent or to both parents. —*plural* **daugh′ ters**

day (dā) *noun*   a period of 24 hours, from midnight to midnight. —*plural* **days**

dear (dir) *adjective*   much loved [He visited his *dear* friend.] —**dear′ er, dear′ est**

de·cay (di kā′) *verb*   to become rotten by the action of bacteria [The fallen apples *decayed* on the ground.] —**de·cayed′, de·cay′ing**

deer (dir) *noun*   a swift-running, hoofed animal. —*plural* **deer**

de·lay (di lā′) *verb*   to put off to a later time [The freight train *delayed* traffic.] —**de·layed′, de·lay′ ing**

de·light·ed (di līt′ id) *adjective*   highly pleased.

de·ny (di nī′) *verb*   to say that something is not true [They *denied* breaking the window.] —**de·nied′, de·ny′ ing**

de·stroy (di stroi′) *verb*   to break up, tear down, or ruin [The flood *destroyed* 300 homes.] —**de·stroyed′, de·stroy′ ing**

did·n't (did′ 'nt) did not.

dig (dig) *verb*   to turn up ground. —**dug, dig′ ging**

din·ner (din′ ər) *noun*   the main meal of the day. —*plural* **din′ ners**

dip (dip) *verb*   to put into a liquid and quickly pull out again [*Dip* the brush into the paint.] —**dipped, dip′ ping**

dip·per (dip′ ər) *noun*   ladle. —*plural* **dip′ pers**

dish (dish) *noun*   any plate or bowl used to serve food. —*plural* **dish′ es**

doc·tor (däk′ tər) *noun*   a person trained to heal the sick. —*plural* **doc′ tors**

does·n't (duz′ 'nt) does not.

dol·lar (däl′ ər) *noun*   a U.S. coin or paper money. —*plural* **dol′ lars**

don·key (dang′ kē *or* dông′ kē) *noun*   an animal like a small horse with long ears. —*plural* **don′ keys**

don't (dōnt) do not.

door·knob (dôr′ näb′) *noun*   a small knob on a door, usually for releasing the latch.

doz·en (duz′ 'n) *noun*   a group of twelve [The carton holds a *dozen* eggs.] —*plural* **doz′ ens**

draw·er (drô′ ər) *noun*   a box that slides in and out of a table, chest, or desk. —*plural* **draw′ ers**

drear·y (drir′ ē) *adjective*   gloomy, sad, or dull [That's such a long, *dreary* tale.] —**drear′ i·er, drear′ i·est**

dress (dres) *noun*   the outer garment worn by girls and women. —*plural* **dress′ es**

dress·er (dres′ ər) *noun*   a chest of drawers for a bedroom [My clothes are folded in the *dresser*.] —*plural* **dress′ ers**

drib·ble (drib′ 'l) *verb*   to control a ball with short bounces or kicks. —**drib′ bled, drib′ bling**

drift (drift) *verb*   to be carried along by a current of water or air [The raft will *drift* downstream.] —**drift′ ed, drift′ ing**

drive (drīv) *verb*   to control a car, bus, or horse. —**drove, driv′ en, driv′ ing**

drop (dräp) *verb* to fall or let fall [He *dropped* his lunch in the mud.] —**dropped, drop′ ping**

drop·per (dräp′ ər) *noun* a small glass tube used to measure out a liquid in drops. —*plural* **drop′ pers**

drum (drum) *noun* an instrument played by beating. —*plural* **drums**

drum·mer (drum′ ər) *noun* a person who plays a drum. —*plural* **drum′ mers**

dry (drī) *verb* to make or become dry. —**dried, dry′ ing**

dur·ing (door′ ing *or* dyoor′ ing) *preposition* throughout the whole time of [Food was hard to get *during* the war.]

du·ty (dōōt′ ē) *noun* any of the things that are supposed to be done. —*plural* **du′ ties**

E

early (ur′ lē) *adverb, adjective* **1** near the beginning; soon after the start [in the *early* afternoon; *early* in his career]. **2** before the usual time [The bus came *early*.] —**ear′ li·er, ear′ li·est**

earn (urn) *verb* to get pay for work done [She *earns* $5 an hour.] —**earned, earn′ ing**

earth (urth) *noun* soil or ground [Farmers seed the *earth*.]

eas·y (ē′ zē) *adjective* not hard to do or learn. —**eas′ i·er, eas′ i·est**

elf (elf) *noun* a small fairy in folk tales. —*plural* **elves**

else (els) *adjective* not the same; other [I thought you were someone *else*.]

em·ploy (im ploi′) *verb* to hire and pay for the work of. —**em·ployed′, em·ploy′ ing**

en·e·my (en′ ə mē) *noun* a person or group who hates or fights another. —*plural* **en′ e·mies**

en·joy (in joi′) *verb* to get pleasure from [We *enjoyed* the ball game.] —**en·joyed′, en·joy′ ing**

e·qual (ē′ kwəl) *adjective* of the same amount, size, or value.

e·rase (i rās′) *verb* to rub out [I had to *erase* my mistake.] —**e·rased′, e·ras′ ing**

e·ras·er (i rā′ sər) *noun* a thing that erases. —*plural* **e·ras′ ers**

er·rand (er′ ənd) *noun* a short trip to do a thing. —*plural* **er′ rands**

e·ven (ē′ vən) *adjective* flat, smooth [This is an *even* surface.]

eve·ning (ēv′ ning) *noun* the close of day and early part of night [The *evening* shadows lengthen as the sun sets.] —*plural* **eve′ nings**

ev·er·y (ev′ rē) *adjective* each [He knows *every* person here.]

ex·plode (ik splōd′) *verb* to blow up with a loud noise [The firecracker *exploded*.] —**ex·plod′ ed, ex·plod′ ing**

F

fall (fôl) *verb* to come down suddenly; tumble. —**fell, fall′ en, fall′ ing**

fam·i·ly (fam′ ə lē) *noun* a group made up of parents and their children. —*plural* **fam′ i·lies**

fas·ten (fas′ 'n) *verb* attach [The collar is *fastened* to the shirt.] —**fas′ ten, fas′ ten·ing**

fa·ther (fä′ thər) *noun* a male parent. —*plural* **fa′ thers**

fear (fir) *noun* the feeling of being near to danger or pain [I have a *fear* of large, barking dogs.] —*plural* **fears**

feed (fēd) *verb* to give food to. —**fed, feed′ ing**

fer·ry (fer′ ē) *noun* a boat used to take people and cars across a river. —*plural* **fer′ ries**

a	fat	ir	here	ou	out	zh	leisure
ā	ape	ī	bite, fire	u	up	ng	ring
ä	car, lot	ō	go	ur	fur		a *in* ago
e	ten	ô	law, horn	ch	chin		e *in* agent
er	care	oi	oil	sh	she	ə =	i *in* unity
ē	even	oo	look	th	thin		o *in* collect
i	hit	ōō	tool	th	then		u *in* focus

fid·dle (fid′ ′l) *noun* a violin. —*plural*
fid′ dles

fight (fīt) *verb* battle; struggle [The children
began to *fight*.] —**fought, fight′ ing**

find (fīnd) *verb* to get back something that has
been lost [We *found* the missing book.]
—**found, find′ ing**

fin·ger (fing′ gər) *noun* any of the five parts at
the end of the hand. —*plural* **fin′ gers**

fire (fīr) *noun* the heat and light of something
burning. —*plural* **fires**

fix (fiks) *verb* to make stay in place. —**fixed,
fix′ ing**

flag (flag) *noun* a piece of cloth with colors and
designs used as a symbol of a country or state.
—*plural* **flags**

flash·light (flash′ līt) *noun* a battery-operated
light that is carried. —*plural* **flash′ lights**

flat (flat) *adjective* smooth and level.
—**flat′ ter, flat′ test**

fli·er (flī′ ər) *noun* a person who flies an
airplane. —*plural* **fli′ ers**

flight (flīt) *noun* a trip through the air [We made
a 500–mile *flight*.] —*plural* **flights**

float (flōt) *verb* to rest on top of water [The raft
floated on the lake.] —**float′ ed, float′ ing**

flood (flud) *noun* an overflowing of water on
land [Heavy rains caused a *flood*.] —*plural*
floods

flour (flour) *noun* grain that has been ground
into a fine powder.

fly (flī) *verb* to move through the air [Birds *fly*
south each winter.] —**flew, flown, fly′ ing**
♦*noun* a flying insect [Swat that *fly*!] —*plural*
flies

fog·gy (fôg′ ē *or* fäg′ ē) *adjective* covered with
fog [It was too *foggy* to see.] —**fog′ gi·er,
fog′ gi·est**

fol·low (fäl′ ō) *verb* to go after [The dog
followed him home.] —**fol′ lowed, fol′ low·ing**

foot (foot) *noun* the end of the leg, on which
one stands or moves. —*plural* **feet**

fore·cast (fôr′ kast) *verb* to tell how something
will turn out; predict [Rain is *forecast* for
tomorrow.] —**fore′ cast** *or* **fore′ cast·ed,
fore′ cast·ing**

for·get (fər get′) *verb* to be unable to remember
[I *forgot* her address.] —**for·got′, for·got′ ten,
for·get′ ting**

fork (fôrk) *noun* a tool with prongs at one end
used to pick up something. —*plural* **forks**

forth (fôrth) *adverb* forward or onward.

foun·tain (foun′ t′n) *noun* a thing built for a
stream of water to rise and fall in [Get a drink at
the *fountain*.] —*plural* **foun′ tains**

fox (fäks) *noun* a small animal with pointed
ears, bushy tail, and reddish fur. —*plural*
fox′ es

freeze (frēz) *verb* to harden into ice. —**froze,
fro′ zen, freez′ ing**

friend (frend) *noun* a person whom one knows
well and likes. —*plural* **friends**

fright·en (frīt′ ′n) *verb* to scare.
—**fright′ ened, fright′ en·ing**

from (frum *or* främ) *preposition* starting at;
out of.

fry (frī) *verb* to cook in hot fat [We *fried*
chicken for dinner.] —**fried, fry′ ing**

full (fool) *adjective* filled [This is a *full* jar.]

fun·ny (fun′ ē) *adjective* causing smiles or
laughter. —**fun′ ni·er, fun′ ni·est**

fur (fʉr) *noun* the soft, thick hair that covers
many animals. —*plural* **furs**

fur·ry (fʉr′ ē) *adjective* covered with fur.
—**fur′ ri·er, fur′ ri·est**

G

gain (gān) *verb* to increase [He *gained* ten pounds in two months.] —**gained, gain′ ing**

gal·lon (gal′ ən) *noun* a measure of liquids equal to four quarts. —*plural* **gal′ lons**

gas (gas) *noun* something that has the same form as the air [Oxygen is a *gas*.] —*plural* **gas′ es**

gear (gir) *noun* part of an arrangement of notched wheels within a machine that pass motion to each other [The *gears* of the car were rusty.] —*plural* **gears**

gig·gle (gig′ ′l) *verb* to laugh in a silly way. —**gig′ gled, gig′ gling**

girl (gʉrl) *noun* a female child. —*plural* **girls**

glass (glas) *noun* **1** a hard substance that lets light through [The windows are made of *glass*.] **2** a container for drinking [Pour milk into my *glass*.] —*plural* **glass′ es**

glove (gluv) *noun* a covering to protect the hand [Surgeons wear rubber *gloves*.] —*plural* **gloves**

glue (glo͞o) *noun* a sticky substance ♦*verb* to stick together with glue [She *glued* the broken plate together.] —**glued, glu′ ing**

go (gō) *verb* to move away; leave. —**went, go′ ing**

goat (gōt) *noun* a cud-chewing animal with horns. —*plural* **goats**

gold·fish (gōld′ fish) *noun* a small, orange fish kept in ponds or fishbowls. —*plural* **gold′ fish**

gone (gôn) *a past form of* **go** moved away; departed.

goose (go͞os) *noun* a swimming bird like a duck but with a longer neck. —*plural* **geese**

grand·fa·ther (gran′ fä′ *th*ər *or* grand′ fä′ *th*ər) *noun* the father of one's father or mother. —*plural* **grand′ fa·thers**

grand·moth·er (gran′ mu*th*′ ər *or* grand′ mu*th*′ ər) *noun* the mother of one's father or mother. —*plural* **grand′ moth′ ers**

grape (grāp) *noun* a small fruit with a smooth skin. —*plural* **grapes**

grease (grēs) *noun* any soft, oily substance.

greas·y (grē′ sē *or* grē′ zē) *adjective* smeared with grease [Look at those *greasy* hands!] —**greas′ i·er, greas′ i·est**

grim·y (grī′ mē) *adjective* very dirty. —**grim′ i·er, grim′ i·est**

grin (grin) *verb* to make a big or foolish smile [The clown *grinned* at us.] —**grinned, grin′ ning**

groan (grōn) *verb* to make a sound showing sadness or pain [We *groaned* when our team lost.] —**groaned, groan′ ing**

ground (ground) *noun* land; earth.

guess (ges) *verb* to judge or decide about something without knowing for certain [Can you *guess* how old he is?] —**guessed, guess′ ing**

H

had·n't (had′ ′nt) had not.

hair (her) *noun* growth that comes from the skin of human beings and some animals [I must comb my *hair*.]

half (haf) *noun* either of the two equal parts of something [Five is *half* of ten.] —*plural* **halves**

ham·burg·er (ham′ bʉr′ gər) *noun* a small, flat patty of ground beef. —*plural* **ham′ burg·ers**

a	fat	ir	here	ou	out	zh	leisure
ā	ape	ī	bite, fire	u	up	ng	ring
ä	car, lot	ō	go	ʉr	fur		a *in* ago
e	ten	ô	law, horn	ch	chin		e *in* agent
er	care	oi	oil	sh	she	ə =	i *in* unity
ē	even	oo	look	th	thin		o *in* collect
i	hit	o͞o	tool	*th*	then		u *in* focus

hap·pen (hap′ ′n) *verb*　to take place, especially by chance [What *happened* at school today?] —**hap′ pened, hap′ pen·ing**

hap·py (hap′ ē) *adjective*　feeling joy and gladness. —**hap′ pi·er, hap′ pi·est**

har·bor (här′ bər) *noun*　a port. —*plural* **har′ bors**

has·n't (haz′ ′nt) has not.

haste (hāst) *noun*　a hurrying in a careless way [*Haste* makes waste.]

hast·y (hās′ tē) *adjective*　done or made too quickly [Don't make a *hasty* decision.] —**hast′ i·er, hast′ i·est**

have (hav) *verb*　to be the owner of [She *has* a car.] —**had, hav′ ing**

health·y (hel′ thē) *adjective*　well [She is a *healthy* child.] —**health′ i·er, health′ i·est**

hear (hir) *verb*　to receive sound through the ears [I *hear* music.] —**heard, hear′ ing**

heart (härt) *noun*　the muscle in the body that moves blood. —*plural* **hearts**

heav·y (hev′ ē) *adjective*　weighing very much [The dog was too *heavy* to carry.] —**heav′ i·er, heav′ i·est**

height (hīt) *noun*　the highest point or degree [The actor reached the *height* of fame.] —*plural* **heights**

he'll (hēl) he will.

herd (hurd) *noun*　a number of cattle living together [They had a *herd* of 100 cows.] —*plural* **herds**

high (hī) *adjective*　tall [That's a very *high* mountain.] —**high′ er, high′ est**

hike (hīk) *verb*　to take a long walk in the woods or country [We *hiked* to the river.] —**hiked, hik′ ing**

hire (hīr) *verb*　to employ [She has *hired* a new secretary.] —**hired, hir′ ing**

hog (hôg *or* häg) *noun*　a pig, especially a full-grown pig raised for meat. —*plural* **hogs**

hold (hōld) *verb*　to take and keep in the hands or arms [Please *hold* the baby for a while.] —**held, hold′ ing**

hol·i·day (häl′ ə dā) *noun*　a day set aside to celebrate some event. —*plural* **hol′ i·days**

hon·ey (hun′ ē) *noun*　a thick, sweet, yellow syrup made by bees [Mother spread *honey* on her roll.]

hop (häp) *verb*　to leap on one foot. —**hopped, hop′ ping**

horn (hôrn) *noun*　**1** a hard, pointed growth on the head of some animals. **2** a brass-wind instrument. —*plural* **horns**

hose (hōz) *noun*　a tube through which fluid is sent [Use the garden *hose*.] —*plural* **hos′ es**

hot (hät) *adjective*　having a high temperature. —**hot′ ter, hot′ test**

hour (our) *noun*　60 minutes. —*plural* **hours**

house (hous) *noun*　a building for people to live in. —*plural* **hous′ es**

how's (houz) how is.

hud·dle (hud′ ′l) *noun*　a huddling together of a football team to get signals for the next play. —*plural* **hud′ dles**

hun·gry (hung′ grē) *adjective*　needing food. —**hun′ gri·er, hun′ gri·est**

hur·ry (hur′ ē) *verb*　to move too quickly [We *hurried* because we were late.] —**hur′ ried, hur′ ry·ing**

hurt (hurt) *verb*　to have pain [My head *hurts*.] —**hurt, hurt′ ing**

I

i·cy (ī′ sē) *adjective*　slippery or very cold [He slipped on the *icy* steps.] —**i′ ci·er, i′ ci·est**

I'd (īd)　**1** I had.　**2** I would.　**3** I should.

inch (inch) *noun*　a unit of measure. —*plural* **inch′ es**

in·side (in′ sīd′) *noun*   the part within [Wash the windows on the *inside*.]

in·vite (in vīt′) *verb*   to ask to be one's guest [I *invited* her to dinner.] —**in·vit′ ed, in·vit′ ing**

I've (īv) I have.

J

jack·et (jak′ it) *noun*   a short coat. —*plural* **jack′ ets**

jour·ney (jʉr′ nē) *noun*   a trip [She took a *journey* around the world.] —*plural* **jour′neys**

jug·gle (jug′ ′l) *verb*   to do tricks with the hands [He can *juggle* three balls at once.] —**jug′ gled, jug′ gling**

K

keep (kēp) *verb*   **1** to have and not let go [*Keep* the change.] **2** to make last or continue [*Keep* your engine running.] —**kept, keep′ ing**

ket·tle (ket′ ′l) *noun*   a teakettle. —*plural* **ket′ tles**

key (kē) *noun*   a small metal device that locks or unlocks a door or drawer. —*plural* **keys**

knap·sack (nap′ sak) *noun*   a bag worn on the back for carrying supplies. —*plural* **knap′ sacks**

knee (nē) *noun*   the joint between the thigh and lower leg. —*plural* **knees**

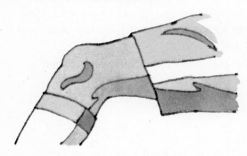

kneel (nēl) *verb*   to rest on a knee or knees [*Kneel* down to tie your shoes.] —**knelt, kneel′ ing**

knife (nīf) *noun*   a cutting tool with a flat, sharp blade. —*plural* **knives**

knot (nät) *verb*   to tie or fasten with a knot. —**knot′ ted, knot′ ting**

know (nō) *verb*   to be aware of; realize [Does he *know* what happened?] —**knew, known, know′ ing**

knuck·le (nuk′ ′l) *noun*   a joint of the finger. —*plural* **knuck′ les**

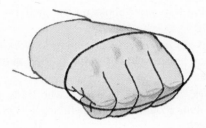

L

lad·der (lad′ ər) *noun*   a frame of two long pieces connected by rungs, used for climbing. —*plural* **lad′ ders**

la·dy (lā′ dē) *noun*   a woman. —*plural* **la′ dies**

lake (lāk) *noun*   a large body of water surrounded by land. —*plural* **lakes**

a	fat	**ir**	here	**ou**	out	**zh**	leisure
ā	ape	**ī**	bite, fire	**u**	up	**ng**	ring
ä	car, lot	**ō**	go	**ʉr**	fur		a *in* ago
e	ten	**ô**	law, horn	**ch**	chin		e *in* agent
er	care	**oi**	oil	**sh**	she	**ə** = i *in* unity
ē	even	**oo**	look	**th**	thin		o *in* collect
i	hit	**o͞o**	tool	**th**	then		u *in* focus

lamb (lam) *noun*   a young sheep. —*plural*
lambs

large (lärj) *adjective*   big [I have a *large* house.]
—**larg′ er, larg′ est**

lat·er (lāt′ ər) *adverb*   after some time [Don't
wait; I'll come *later*.]

lay (lā) *verb*   to put down to rest on or in
something [*Lay* your books on the shelf.] —**laid,
lay′ ing**

la·zy (lā′ zē) *adjective*   not willing to work hard
[The *lazy* horse wouldn't move.] —**la′ zi·er,
la′ zi·est**

lead·er (lē′ dər) *noun*   a person who leads or
guides [Our scout *leader* likes hiking.] —*plural*
lead′ ers

leaf (lēf) *noun*   a flat green part growing from
the stem of a plant or tree. —*plural* **leaves**

learn (lʉrn) *verb*   to get some knowledge or skill
[I have *learned* to knit.] —**learned, learn′ ing**

leave (lēv) *verb*   **1** to go away from [When did
they *leave* the party?] **2** to let stay [*Leave* the
door open.] —**left, leav′ ing**

leg (leg) *noun*   part of the body used for standing
and walking. —*plural* **legs**

lem·on·ade (lem ə nād′) *noun*   a drink made of
lemon juice, sugar, and water.

les·son (les′ 'n) *noun*   something to be learned
by a student [She studied her math *lesson*.]
—*plural* **les′ sons**

let's (lets) let us.

life (līf) *noun*   the time that a person or thing is
alive [Her *life* has just begun.] —*plural* **lives**

light (līt) *noun*   **1** brightness [Is there enough
light in this room?] **2** something that gives light,
as a lamp [The room looked cheerful with the
light on.] —*plural* **lights**

light·ning (līt′ ning) *noun*   a flash of light in the
sky.

limb (lim) *noun*   **1** an arm, leg, or wing. **2** a
large branch of a tree. —*plural* **limbs**

lit·tle (lit′ 'l) *adjective*   small in size [We live in
a *little* house.] —**lit′ tler, lit′ tlest**

live (liv) *verb*   to make one's home [We *live* on
a farm.] —**lived, liv′ ing**

load (lōd) *noun*   something that is carried at one
time [He carried the heavy *load*.] —*plural*
loads

loaf (lōf) *noun*   bread baked in one piece.
—*plural* **loaves**

loan (lōn) *verb*   to lend something to be returned
[I *loaned* him a dime.] —**loaned, loan′ ing**

log (lôg) *noun*   a part of a tree that has been cut
down [We cut up *logs* for the fire.] —*plural*
logs

loud (loud) *adjective*   strong in sound [Can you
hear that *loud* noise?] —**loud′ er, loud′ est**

luck·y (luk′ ē) *adjective*   having good luck [She
was *lucky* to win the contest.] —**luck′ i·er,
luck′ i·est**

lunch (lunch) *noun*   the meal eaten between
breakfast and dinner. —*plural* **lunch′ es**

M

man (man) *noun*   an adult male human being.
—*plural* **men**

mar·ry (mar′ ē) *verb*   to take someone as
husband or wife. —**mar′ ried, mar′ ry·ing**

may·be (mā′ bē) *adverb*   perhaps.

melt (melt) *verb*   to change from a solid to a liquid, as by heat [The sun *melted* the snow.] —**melt′ ed, melt′ ing**

mid·dle (mid′ ′l) *noun*   the point that is halfway between the ends or in the center [The island is in the *middle* of the lake.]

mid·night (mid′ nīt) *noun*   twelve o'clock at night.

might (mīt) *noun*   great strength or power [Pull with all your *might*.]

mile (mīl) *noun*   a measure of length equal to 5,280 feet. —*plural* **miles**

milk (milk) *noun*   a white liquid used for drinking [I poured *milk* on my cereal.]

mil·lion (mil′ yən) *noun, adjective*   a thousand thousands. —*plural* **mil′ lions**

mind (mīnd) *noun*   intellect [The *mind* was once thought of as apart from the body.] —*plural* **minds**

min·ute (min′ it) *noun*   a period of time; 60 seconds [Turn off the oven in ten *minutes*.] —*plural* **min′ utes**

mon·key (mung′ kē) *noun*   any animal of the group that appears most like man. —*plural* **mon′ keys**

month (munth) *noun*   any of the twelve parts into which the year is divided [Thanksgiving comes in the *month* of November.] —*plural* **months**

more (môr) *adjective*   greater in amount or degree [He has *more* free time than I do.]

morn·ing (môr′ ning) *noun*   the early part of the day [Joe slept late this *morning*.]

moss (môs) *noun*   tiny green plants growing in clumps like velvet [*Moss* covered the rock.]

moth·er (mu*th*′ ər) *noun*   a female parent —*plural* **moth′ ers**

moun·tain (moun′ t′n) *noun*   a very high hill [We climbed a steep *mountain*.] —*plural* **moun′ tains**

mouse (mous) *noun*   a small, gnawing animal. —*plural* **mice**

mouth (mouth) *noun*   the opening in the head for eating and making sounds [The soup burned my *mouth*.] —*plural* **mouths**

move (mo̅o̅v) *verb*   **1** to change place or position [*Move* the picture to the left.] **2** to change the place where one lives [They *moved* to New York.] —**moved, mov′ ing**

mud·dy (mud′ ē) *adjective*   full of mud [Clean your *muddy* boots.] —**mud′ di·er, mud′ di·est**

mul·ti·ply (mul′ tə plī) *verb*   to repeat a figure a certain number of times [She *multiplied* 3 by 4 to get 12.] —**mul′ ti·plied, mul′ ti·ply·ing**

N

nap·kin (nap′ kin) *noun*   a piece of cloth or paper used while eating to protect clothes or to wipe fingers or lips. —*plural* **nap′ kins**

near (nir) *adjective*   not far; close [Our house is *near* to the school.] —**near′ er, near′ est**

neigh·bor (nā′ bər) *noun*   a person who lives near another. —*plural* **neigh′ bors**

a	fat	ir	here	ou	out	zh	leisure
ā	ape	ī	bite, fire	u	up	ng	ring
ä	car, lot	ō	go	ʉr	fur		a *in* ago
e	ten	ô	law, horn	ch	chin		e *in* agent
er	care	oi	oil	sh	she	ə =	i *in* unity
ē	even	oo	look	th	thin		o *in* collect
i	hit	o̅o̅	tool	*th*	then		u *in* focus

neph·ew (nef′ yoō) *noun* the son of one's brother or sister. —*plural* **neph′ ews**

nev·er (nev′ ər) *adverb* not ever [I *never* saw her again.]

new (noō) *adjective* that has not been worn or used [We sell *new* and used cars.] —**new′ er, new′ est**

news·pa·per (noōz′ pā′ pər) *noun* publication containing news, ideas, and advertisements. —*plural* **news′ pa′ pers**

nib·ble (nib′ ′l) *noun* a small bite. —*plural* **nib′ bles**

niece (nēs) *noun* the daughter of one's brother or sister. —*plural* **niec′ es**

night (nīt) *noun* the time of darkness between sunset and sunrise. —*plural* **nights**

noise (noiz) *noun* a loud, harsh sound [Listen to the *noise* of the fireworks.] —*plural* **nois′ es**

nois·y (noi′ zē) *adjective* making noise [The class is too *noisy*.] —**nois′ i·er, nois′ i·est**

none (nun) *pronoun* no one. [*None* of us is ready.]

north (nôrth) *noun* the direction to the right of a person facing the sunset.

numb (num) *adjective* not able to feel [My toes were *numb* with cold.] —**numb′ er, numb′ est**

num·ber (num′ bər) *noun* a symbol or word used in counting or that tells how many [Two, 7, and tenth are all *numbers*.] —*plural* **num′ bers**

nurse (nʉrs) *noun* a person trained to care for sick people. —*plural* **nurs′ es**

O

oak (ōk) *noun* a large tree with hard wood and nuts called acorns. —*plural* **oaks**

oat (ōt) *noun* a cereal grass whose grain is used as food. —*plural* **oats**

o·bey (ō bā′) *verb* to carry out the orders of [Our dog *obeys* our commands.] —**o·beyed′, o·bey′ ing**

once (wuns) *adverb* one time. [We eat together *once* a week.]

o·pen (ō′ p'n) *verb* to make or become open [Please *open* that trunk.] —**o′ pened, o′ pen·ing**

or·der (ôr′ dər) *noun* a direction telling someone what to do [The general gave his troops an *order*.] ♦*verb* to tell someone what to do [The police officer *ordered* the crowd to move.] —**or′ dered, or′ der·ing**

out (out) *adverb* away from the inside or center [Come *out* and play.]

out·doors (out′ dôrz′) *adverb* in the open; outside [We ran *outdoors* to play.]

out·fit (out′ fit) *noun* clothing used in some activity [Wear a hiking *outfit*.] —*plural* **out′ fits**

out·side (out′ sīd′) *adverb* on or to the outside [Let's play *outside*.]

o·ver (ō′ vər) *preposition* in, at, or to a place above [Hang the picture *over* the fireplace.]

o·ver·sleep (ō vər slēp′) *verb* to sleep past the time one meant to get up [Lisa *overslept* today.] —**o·ver·slept′, o·ver·sleep′ ing**

ox (äks) *noun* a male of the cattle family. —*plural* **oxen**

P

pail (pāl) *noun* a round, deep container for holding and carrying liquids. —*plural* **pails**

paint·er (pānt′ ər) *noun* an artist who paints pictures. —*plural* **paint′ ers**

pair (per) *noun*   a set of two [I have a new *pair* of skates.]

pa·per (pā′ pər) *noun*   a thin material used to write on. —*plural* **pa′ pers**

par·ty (pär′ tē) *noun*   a gathering of people to have fun. —*plural* **par′ ties**

pass (pas) *verb*   to go by [I *passed* your house today.] —**passed, pass′ ing**

paste (pāst) *noun*   a mixture used for sticking paper or other things together. ◆*verb*   to make stick [Let's *paste* pictures in this book.] —**past′ ed, past′ ing**

pear (per) *noun*   a soft, yellow or green juicy fruit. —*plural* **pears**

pearl (purl) *noun*   a hard, round stone formed inside oysters and often used in jewelry. —*plural* **pearls**

pen·ny (pen′ ē) *noun*   a cent. —*plural* **pen′ nies**

pep·per (pep′ ər) *noun*   a hot-tasting seasoning.

per·haps (pər haps′) *adverb*   possibly; maybe [*Perhaps* it will rain.]

per·son (pur′ s'n) *noun*   a human being [I know every *person* in this room.] —*plural* **per′ sons**

pic·nic (pik′ nik) *noun*   a meal eaten outdoors [We will have our *picnic* in the park.] —*plural* **pic′ nics**

pic·ture (pik′ chər) *noun*   a drawing, painting, or photograph. —*plural* **pic′ tures**

pile (pīl) *noun*   a mass of things heaped together [We made a big *pile* of leaves.] —*plural* **piles**

pin (pin) *noun*   a thin, sharp wire used to fasten things. ◆*verb*   to fasten with a pin [He *pinned* the badge to his sweater.] —**pinned, pin′ ning**

pint (pīnt) *noun*   a measure of volume equal to ½ quart. —*plural* **pints**

pitch·er (pich′ ər) *noun*   the baseball player who pitches the balls to the batters. —*plural* **pitch′ ers**

place (plās) *noun*   a city, town, or village. —*plural* **plac′ es**

plan (plan) *verb*   to think of a way of making or doing something [We *planned* our party.] —**planned, plan′ ning**

plant (plant) *noun*   a living thing that makes its own food [Many *plants* were growing in the garden.] ◆*verb*   to put into the ground to grow [We *planted* corn in our yard.] —**plant′ ed, plant′ ing**

play (plā) *verb*   to have fun [Children like to *play* outdoors.] —**played, play′ ing** ◆*noun*   a story acted out on stage, radio, or television [They went to see a *play*.] —*plural* **plays**

play·ground (plā′ ground) *noun*   a place for outdoor games and play. —*plural* **play′ grounds**

plumb·er (plum′ ər) *noun*   a person who repairs water and gas pipes. —*plural* **plumb′ ers**

po·ny (pō′ nē) *noun*   a type of small horse. —*plural* **po′ nies**

pour (pôr) *verb*   to let flow in a steady stream [The milk was *poured* into glasses.] —**poured, pour′ ing**

praise (prāz) *verb*   to say good things about [My teacher *praised* my work.] —**praised, prais′ ing**

press (pres) *verb*   to put steady weight on [He *pressed* the doorbell.] —**pressed, press′ ing**

pret·ty (prit′ ē *or* pur′ tē) *adjective*   nice to look at or hear. —**pret′ ti·er, pret′ ti·est**

price (prīs) *noun*   the cost of something. —*plural* **pric′ es**

prin·cess (prin′ sis) *noun*   daughter of a king or queen. —*plural* **prin′ ces·ses**

a	fat	ir	here	ou	out	zh	leisure
ā	ape	ī	bite, fire	u	up	ng	ring
ä	car, lot	ō	go	ur	fur		a *in* ago
e	ten	ô	law, horn	ch	chin		e *in* agent
er	care	oi	oil	sh	she	ə =	i *in* unity
ē	even	oo	look	th	thin		o *in* collect
i	hit	oo	tool	th	then		u *in* focus

prize (prīz) *noun*   something given to a winner of a contest [The *prize* is a blue ribbon.] —*plural* **priz′ es**

prog·ress (präg′ res) *noun*   a developing or improving [She shows *progress* in learning French.] ◆*verb*   (prə gres′) to move forward. —**pro·gressed′, pro·gress′ ing**

pry (prī) *verb*   to raise or move with a lever or crowbar. —**pried, pry′ ing**

pud·dle (pud′ ′l) *noun*   a small pool of water [Stay out of the *puddles* after the rain.] —*plural* **pud′ dles**

pull (pool) *verb*   to move or draw closer [*Pull* up your socks.] —**pulled, pull′ ing**

pump·kin (pum′ kin *or* pung′ kin) *noun*   a large, round, orange fruit that grows on a vine. —*plural* **pump′ kins**

pup·py (pup′ ē) *noun*   a young dog. —*plural* **pup′ pies**

puz·zle (puz′ ′l) *noun*   a toy or problem that tests one's cleverness or skill [Let's put the jigsaw *puzzle* together.] —*plural* **puz′ zles**

R

race (rās) *noun*   a contest of speed [Her horse won the *race*.] —*plural* **rac′ es**   ◆ *verb*   to have a race with [I'll *race* you to the corner.] —**raced, rac′ ing**

rad·ish (rad′ ish) *noun*   a sharp-tasting root which is eaten raw. —*plural* **rad′ ish·es**

rain (rān) *noun*   water that falls to the earth in drops. ◆*verb*   to fall as rain [It is *raining*.] —**rained, rain′ ing**

rain·coat (rān′ kōt) *noun*   a waterproof coat. —*plural* **rain′ coats**

rain·y (rā′ nē) *adjective*   having much rain [Ball games are cancelled on *rainy* days.] —**rain′ i·er, rain′ i·est**

ranch (ranch) *noun*   a large farm for raising cattle, horses, or sheep. —*plural* **ranch′ es**

rat·tle (rat′ ′l) *noun*   a baby's toy that rattles when shaken. —*plural* **rat′ tles**

ray (rā) *noun*   a narrow beam of light [The *rays* of the flashlight are bright.] —*plural* **rays**

rear (rir) *adjective*   at or in the back part [Please deliver groceries to the *rear* door.]

re·bound (ri bound′) *verb*   to bounce back [Aaron caught the ball as it *rebounded* from the fence.] —**re·bound′ ed, re·bound′ ing** ◆ (rē′ bound)   **1** a bouncing or bounding back. **2** an object that bounces back.

re·build (rē bild′) *verb*   to build again. —**re·built′, re·build′ ing**

rec·ord (rek′ ərd) *noun*   a disc on which sound has been recorded. —*plural* **rec′ ords**

re·fill (rē fil′) *verb*   to fill again. —**re·filled′, re·fill′ ing**

re·gain (ri gān′) *verb*   to get back again [He *regained* his health slowly.] —**re·gained′, re·gain′ ing**

re·hearse (ri hʉrs′) *verb*   to practice a play or speech. —**re·hearsed′, re·hears′ ing**

re·heat (rē hēt′) *verb*   to make warm again [The cook will *reheat* the soup.] —**re·heat′ ed, re·heat′ ing**

re·mind (ri mīnd′) *verb*   to make remember [*Remind* me to pay the gas bill.] —**re·mind′ ed, re·mind′ ing**

re·new (ri noo′) *verb*   to make new or fresh again [*Renew* that old table by painting it.] —**re·newed′, re·new′ ing**

re·paint (rē pānt′) *verb*   to paint again. —**re·paint′ ed, re·paint′ ing**

re·pay (ri pā′) *verb*   to pay back [Always *repay* a loan.] —**re·paid′, re·pay′ ing**

re·place (ri plās′) *verb* to put another in the place of something used, lost, or broken [*Replace* the worn tire.] —**re·placed′, re·plac′ ing**

re·ply (ri plī′) *verb* to answer [*Reply* to my question.] —**re·plied′, re·ply′ ing**

re·print (rē print′) *verb* to publish again. —**re·print′ ed, re·print′ ing**

re·read (rē rēd′) *verb* to read again. —**re·read′, re·read′ ing**

re·take (rē tāk′) *verb* to take again or take back. —**re·took′, re·tak′ en, re·tak′ ing**

re·teach (rē tēch′) *verb* to teach again. —**re·taught′, re·teach′ ing**

re·tell (rē tel′) *verb* to report or tell a story again. —**re·told′, re·tell′ ing**

re·think (rē think′) *verb* to think over again [We had better *rethink* our plans.] —**re·thought′, re·think′ ing**

re·turn (ri turn′) *verb* to go or send back [I will *return* this sweater.] —**re·turned′, re·turn′ ing**

re·view (ri vyoo′) *verb* to go over or study again [I have to *review* for the math test.] —**re·viewed′, re·view′ ing**

re·vis·it (rē viz′ it) *verb* to visit again. —**re·vis′ it·ed, re·vis′ it·ing**

re·wind (rē wind′) *verb* to wind again [Please *rewind* the hose.] —**re·wound′, re·wind′ ing**

re·write (rē rīt′) *verb* to write again or in different words [An author may *rewrite* a story several times.] —**re·wrote′, re·writ′ ing**

rib·bon (rib′ ən) *noun* a narrow strip used for tying or decorating things [He tied a red *ribbon* on the gift.] —*plural* **rib′ bons**

rid·dle (rid′ ′l) *noun* a puzzle with a tricky meaning or an answer that is hard to guess. —*plural* **rid′ dles**

ride (rīd) *verb* to sit on and make move [I like to *ride* horses.] —**rode, rid′ den, rid′ ing**

right (rīt) *adjective* **1** correct or true [That is the *right* way to go.] **2** opposite of left [Raise your *right* hand.]

ripe (rīp) *adjective* ready to be gathered and used for food. —**rip′ er, rip′ est**

rise (rīz) *verb* to move toward a higher place [The sun is *rising*.] —**rose, ris′ en, ris′ ing**

riv·er (riv′ ər) *noun* a large stream of water [The *river* flowed into the ocean.] —*plural* **riv′ ers**

road (rōd) *noun* highway. —*plural* **roads**

road·way (rōd′ wā) *noun* the part of the road on which cars and trucks travel [The truck blocked the *roadway*.] —*plural* **road′ ways**

roast (rōst) *verb* to cook in an oven or over a fire [We *roasted* a turkey.] —**roast′ ed, roast′ ing**

roll (rōl) *verb* to move by turning over and over [The dog *rolled* on the grass.] —**rolled, roll′ ing** ◆*noun* bread baked in a small, shaped piece. —*plural* **rolls**

roost·er (roos′ tər) a male chicken. [The *rooster* crowed at dawn.] —*plural* **roost′ ers**

round (round) *adjective* shaped like a ball or circle [The earth is *round*.]

run·way (run′ wā) *noun* a long strip of land on which airplanes take off and land. —*plural* **run′ ways**

S

sad (sad) *adjective* causing an unhappy feeling [They cried at the *sad* news.] —**sad′ der, sad′ dest**

a	fat	**ir**	here	**ou**	out	**zh**	leisure
ā	ape	**ī**	bite, fire	**u**	up	**ng**	ring
ä	car, lot	**ō**	go	**ur**	fur		a *in* ago
e	ten	**ô**	law, horn	**ch**	chin		e *in* agent
er	care	**oi**	oil	**sh**	she	**ə** =	i *in* unity
ē	even	**oo**	look	**th**	thin		o *in* collect
i	hit	**oo**	tool	**th**	then		u *in* focus

sad·dle (sad′ ′l) *noun* a seat for a rider on a horse. —*plural* **sad′ dles**

salt·y (sôl′ tē) *adjective* tasting of salt [Pretzels are *salty*.] —**salt′ i·er, salt′ i·est**

sand·y (san′ dē) *adjective* full of sand [That is a *sandy* shore.] —**sand′ i·er, sand′ i·est**

save (sāv) *verb* **1** to rescue [He was *saved* from drowning.] **2** to keep or store up [She *saves* bottle caps.] —**saved, sav′ ing**

say (sā) *verb* to speak [Can this parrot *say* its name?] —**said, say′ ing**

scis·sors (siz′ ərz) *noun plural* a two-bladed tool used for cutting.

scout (skout) *verb* to look for something [The campers *scouted* for firewood.] —**scout′ed, scout′ ing**

scrape (skrāp) *verb* to rub the surface or skin from [He fell and *scraped* his knee.] —**scraped, scrap′ ing**

scrib·ble (skrib′ ′l) *verb* to write quickly or carelessly. —**scrib′ bled, scrib′ bling**

scur·ry (skʉr′ ē) *verb* to run quickly; scamper. —**scur′ ried, scur′ ry·ing**

search (sʉrch) *verb* to look in order to find something [We *searched* the house.] —**searched, search′ ing**

see (sē) *verb* to look; to use one's sight [I need glasses to *see* well.] —**saw, seen, see′ ing**

send (send) *verb* to cause to go or be carried [*Send* them home for their lunch.] —**sent, send′ ing**

set·tle (set′ ′l) *verb* to come to an agreement or decision [We *settled* our argument.] —**set′ tled, set′ tling**

shad·y (shād′ ē) *adjective* shaded from the sun [It was *shady* in the forest.] —**shad′ i·er, shad′ i·est**

shall (shal) *helping verb* [I *shall* leave tomorrow.]

share (sher) *verb* to divide and give out [She *shared* her candy with us.] —**shared, shar′ ing**

she'd (shēd) **1** she had. **2** she would.

sheep (shēp) *noun* a cud-chewing animal that is covered with wool. —*plural* **sheep**

shelf (shelf) *noun* a thin, flat length of wood or metal used to hold things [Put the book on the top *shelf*.] —*plural* **shelves**

shell (shel) *noun* a hard outer covering, as on eggs or clams. —*plural* **shells**

sher·iff (sher′ if) *noun* the chief officer of the law in a county. —*plural* **sher′ iffs**

shin·y (shīn′ ē) *adjective* bright; shining [The child found a *shiny* stone.] —**shin′ i·er, shin′ i·est**

shop·per (shöp′ ər) *noun* one who shops. — *plural* **shop′ pers**

shorts (shôrts) *noun plural* short pants that end above the knee.

should·n't (shood′ ′nt) should not

shout (shout) *verb* to say in a loud voice [They *shouted* out the cheer.] —**shout′ ed, shout′ ing**

side·walk (sīd′ wôk) *noun* a paved path for walking. —*plural* **side′ walks**

sigh (sī) *noun* a long, noisy breath [The sad man gave a deep *sigh*.] —*plural* **sighs**

sight (sīt) *noun* **1** something worth seeing [The Grand Canyon is a *sight* to remember.] —*plural* **sights 2** vision; eyesight [Glasses improved my *sight*.]

since (sins) *adverb* from then until now [Lynn came Monday and has been here ever *since*.]

sip (sip) *verb* to drink a little at a time [She *sipped* the hot cocoa.] —**sipped, sip′ ping**

sis·ter (sis′ tər) *noun* a girl or woman as she is related to the other children of her parents. —*plural* **sis′ ters**

size (sīz) *noun* how large or how small a thing is [What *size* is this shirt?] —*plural* **siz′ es**

skat·er (skāt′ ər) *noun* a person who moves on ice skates or roller skates. —*plural* **skat′ ers**

skip (skip) *verb* to move by hopping on first one foot and then the other. —**skipped, skip′ ping**

slam (slam) *verb* to shut with force and noise [Please don't *slam* the door.] —**slammed, slam′ ming**

sleep·y (slēp′ ē) *adjective* drowsy. —**sleep′ i·er, sleep′ i·est**

slice (slīs) *verb* to cut into thin pieces [He *sliced* a loaf of bread.] —**sliced, slic′ ing**

slight (slīt) *adjective* not great or important [There will be a *slight* change in plans.]

small (smôl) *adjective* little in size [I'd like a *small* scoop of ice cream.] —**small′ er, small′ est**

smile (smīl) *verb* to show that one is pleased or happy by making the corners of the mouth turn up. —**smiled, smil′ ing**

smoke (smōk) *noun* the gas and bits of carbon that rise from something burning [*Smoke* rose from the campfire.]

smok·y (smō′ kē) *adjective* filled with smoke [The air looked gray in the *smoky* room.] —**smok′ i·er, smok′ i·est**

sniff (snif) *verb* to smell by pulling air through the nose [He *sniffed* the sour milk.] —**sniffed, sniff′ ing**

soak (sōk) *verb* to make wet by keeping in water [She *soaked* the sponge.] —**soaked, soak′ ing**

soap (sōp) *noun* a substance used with water to wash things.

some·one (sum′ wun) *pronoun* a certain person not named [*Someone* left the door open.]

some·times (sum′ tīmz) *adverb* occasionally [*Sometimes* we go to plays.]

sor·ry (sär′ ē) *adjective* full of sadness or pity [I'm *sorry* you got hurt.] —**sor′ ri·er, sor′ ri·est**

sound (sound) *noun* any noise that can be heard [I hear the *sound* of her footsteps.] —*plural* **sounds**

south (south) *noun* the direction to the left of a person facing the sunset.

spar·row (spar′ ō) *noun* a small gray and brown bird [A *sparrow* sang in the garden.] —*plural* **spar′ rows**

speak (spēk) *verb* talk [They *spoke* to each other on the phone.] —**spoke, speak′ ing**

speak·er (spē′ kər) *noun* a person who speaks or makes speeches. —*plural* **speak′ ers**

spear (spir) *noun* weapon made of a long handle and a sharp point. —*plural* **spears**

spell (spel) *verb* to say or write in order the letters that make up a word [Can you *spell* "seize"?] —**spelled, spell′ ing**

spend (spend) *verb* to pay out or give up [He *spent* $50 for food.] —**spent, spend′ ing**

spin (spin) *verb* to whirl around swiftly [*Spin* the wheel.] —**spun, spin′ ning**

spin·ner (spin′ ər) *noun* a person, animal, or thing that spins [The spider is a *spinner* of webs.] —*plural* **spin′ ners**

a	fat	ir	here	ou	out	zh	leisure
ā	ape	ī	bite, fire	u	up	ng	ring
ä	car, lot	ō	go	ʉr	fur		a *in* ago
e	ten	ô	law, horn	ch	chin		e *in* agent
er	care	oi	oil	sh	she	ə =	i *in* unity
ē	even	oo	look	th	thin		o *in* collect
i	hit	ōo	tool	*th*	then		u *in* focus

sport (spôrt) *noun*   an active game for exercise or fun [Skiing is a winter *sport*.] —*plural* **sports**

spray (sprā) *verb*   to shoot out in a mist of tiny drops [She *sprayed* water on the plants.] —**sprayed, spray′ ing**

spy (spī) *noun*   a person who watches others secretly [The *spy* peered through the window.] —*plural* **spies** ◆*verb*   to act as a spy [Detectives *spied* on him.] —**spied, spy′ ing**

squeak (skwēk) *noun*   a short, high cry or sound [Do you hear the *squeak* of a mouse?] —*plural* **squeaks** ◆*verb*   to make a squeak [His new shoes *squeaked*.] —**squeaked, squeak′ ing**

squeak·y (skwēk′ ē) *adjective*   having a high sound. —**squeak′ i·er, squeak′ i·est**

squeeze (skwēz) *verb*   to press hard [He *squeezed* the sponge dry.] —**squeezed, squeez′ ing**

stack (stak) *verb*   to arrange in a pile [The books were *stacked* on the table.] **stacked, stack′ ing**

sta·ple (stā′ p'l) *noun*   a piece of metal driven into a surface to hold something in place. —*plural* **sta′ ples** ◆*verb*   to fasten with a staple or staples. —**sta′ pled, sta′ pling**

sta·pler (stā′ plər) *noun*   a device for driving staples. —*plural* **sta′ plers**

star (stär) *noun*   a heavenly body seen as a small point of light in the night sky. —*plural* **stars**

star·ry (stär′ē) *adjective*   full of stars [Isn't there a *starry* sky tonight?] —**star′ ri·er, star′ ri·est**

stay (stā) *verb*   remain. [*Stay* at home.] —**stayed, stay′ ing**

steal (stēl) *verb*   to take away something that does not belong to one. —**stole, stol′ en, steal′ ing**

step (step) *noun*   a place to rest the foot in going up or down. —*plural* **steps**

still (stil) *adverb*   until then or now [Is she *still* talking?]

sting (sting) *verb*   to hurt by pricking [Bees can *sting* you.] —**stung, sting′ ing**

stir (stʉr) *verb*   to mix with a spoon or a fork [*Stir* the paint well.] —**stirred, stir′ ring**

stone (stōn) *noun*   rock [That monument is built of *stone*.] —*plural* **stones**

stop (stäp) *verb*   to halt or keep from going on [*Stop* the car.] —**stopped, stop′ ping**

storm (stôrm) *noun*   a strong wind with rain, snow, or lightning [The *storm* knocked down the telephone lines.] —*plural* **storms**

sto·ry (stôr′ ē) *noun*   a telling of some true or made-up happening [Can you tell the *story* of the first Thanksgiving?] —*plural* **sto′ ries**

stray (strā) *noun*   a lost person or animal [We fed the *stray* some dog food.] —*plural* **strays** ◆*verb*   to wander away [Don't *stray* from camp.] —**strayed, stray′ ing**

stud·y (stud′ ē) *verb*   to read so as to understand and remember [*Study* your lessons.] —**stud′ ied, stud′ y·ing**

sub·way (sub′ wā) *noun*   an underground railway [He rode the *subway* downtown.] —*plural* **sub′ ways**

sudden (sud′ 'n) *adjective*   not expected [A *sudden* storm came up.] —**sud′ den·ly** *adverb*

suit·case (sōōt′ kās) *noun*   a case for carrying belongings when traveling. —*plural* **suit′ cas·es**

sum·mer (sum′ ər) *noun*   the warmest season of the year. —*plural* **sum′ mers**

sun·ny (sun′ ē) *adjective*   bright with sunlight. —**sun′ ni·er, sun′ ni·est**

sup·per (sup′ ər) *noun*   the last meal of the day. —*plural* **sup′ pers**

sup·pli·er (sə plī′ ər) *noun*   one who supplies. —*plural* **sup·pli′ ers**

sup·ply (sə plī′) *verb*   to give what is needed [The camp *supplies* sheets and towels.] —**sup·plied′, sup·ply′ing**

sur·vey (sʉr′ vā) *noun* a general study [The *survey* shows that we need more schools.] —*plural* **sur′ veys**

swal·low (swäl′ ō) *verb* to let food or drink go through the throat to the stomach [She *swallowed* the peanut.] —**swal′ lowed, swal′ low·ing**

sway (swā) *verb* to swing or bend from side to side [Grass *swayed* in the wind.] —**swayed, sway′ ing**

sweat·er (swet′ ər) *noun* a knitted garment with sleeves. —*plural* **sweat′ ers**

sweep (swēp) *verb* to clean by brushing with a broom [*Sweep* the floor.] —**swept, sweep′ ing**

swim (swim) *verb* to move in water by using arms and legs [I love to *swim* in the lake.] —**swam, swum, swim′ ming**

swim·mer (swim′ ər) *noun* a person who swims. —*plural* **swim′ mers**

T

tag (tag) *verb* to touch in the game of tag. —**tagged, tag′ ging**

take (tāk) *verb* to get hold of; grasp [*Take* my hand as we cross the street.] —**took, tak′ en, tak′ ing**

talk (tôk) *verb* speak [The baby is learning to *talk*.] —**talked, talk′ ing**

tame (tām) *adjective* no longer wild [Would you like a *tame* skunk?] —**tam′er, tam′est**

tear (ter) *verb* to rip or pull apart [*Tear* the paper into bits.] —**tore, torn, tear′ ing**

tease (tēz) *verb* to bother [They *teased* my dog.] —**teased, teas′ ing**

ten·nis (ten′ is) *noun* a game in which players hit a ball back and forth over a net with rackets.

that's (*th*ats) that is.

them·selves (*th*em selvz′) *pronoun* their own selves [They hurt *themselves*.]

there·fore (*th*er′ fôr) *adverb* for this or that reason.

they'd (*th*ād) **1** they had. **2** they would.

thief (thēf) *noun* a person who steals. —*plural* **thieves**

thigh (thī) *noun* the part of the leg between the knee and hip. —*plural* **thighs**

think (thingk) to use the mind [*Think* before you act.] —**thought, think′ ing**

thorn (thôrn) *noun* a sharp point growing out of a plant stem. —*plural* **thorns**

throat (thrōt) *noun* the upper part of the passage from the mouth to the stomach [I have a sore *throat*.] —*plural* **throats**

thumb (thum) *noun* the short, thick finger nearest the wrist. —*plural* **thumbs**

thun·der (thun′ dər) *noun* the loud noise that comes after lightning.

tie (tī) *verb* to make a knot or bow [He *tied* his necktie.] —**tied, ty′ ing**

tight (tīt) *adjective* fitting too closely [My shirt is too *tight*.] —**tight′ er, tight′ est**

tip (tip) *verb* to overturn; upset. —**tipped, tip′ ping**

tire¹ (tīr) *noun* an air-filled rubber tube that fits around a wheel. —*plural* **tires**

tire² (tīr) *verb* exhaust [The hike *tired* me.] —**tired, tir′ ing**

a	fat	ir	here	ou	out	zh	leisure
ā	ape	ī	bite, fire	u	up	ng	ring
ä	car, lot	ō	go	ʉr	fur		a *in* ago
e	ten	ô	law, horn	ch	chin		e *in* agent
er	care	oi	oil	sh	she	ə =	i *in* unity
ē	even	oo	look	th	thin		o *in* collect
i	hit	o͞o	tool	*th*	then		u *in* focus

toad (tōd) *noun*   a small frog-like animal that lives on land. —*plural* **toads**

toast (tōst) *noun*   bread that has been browned by heating.

to·mor·row (tə mär′ ō *or* tə môr′ ō) *noun*   the day after today.

to·night (tə nīt′) *noun*   this night.

tooth (tōōth) *noun*   white, bony part in the jaw used for biting and chewing. —*plural* **teeth**

tor·na·do (tôr nā′ dō) *noun*   a funnel-shaped column of air that usually destroys everything in its path. —*plural* **tor·na′ does** *or* **tor·na′ dos**

toss (tôs) *verb*   to throw easily [*Toss* the ball here.] —**tossed, toss′ ing**

toy (toi) *noun*   a thing to play with. —*plural* **toys**

trace (trās) *verb*   to copy a picture by following its lines on thin paper placed over it [She *traced* that drawing from a book.] —**traced, trac′ ing**

tray (trā) *noun*   a flat piece of wood or metal for carrying food. —*plural* **trays**

trunk (trungk) *noun*   a large, strong box for storing things or holding clothes while traveling [I packed my clothes in the *trunk*.] —*plural* **trunks**

try (trī) *verb*   attempt [We must *try* to help him.] —**tried, try′ ing**

tur·key (tʉr′ kē) *noun*   a large bird with a small head and spreading tail. —*plural* **tur′ keys**

tur·nip (tʉr′ nip) *noun*   a plant with a round, white or yellow root that is eaten as a vegetable. —*plural* **tur′ nips**

twi·light (twī′ līt) *noun*   the dim light just after sunset.

twin (twin) *noun*   either of two born at the same time to the same mother [Bob and Betty are *twins*.] —*plural* **twins**

U

um·brel·la (um brel′ ə) *noun*   cloth or plastic stretched over a frame at the top of a stick, used to protect one from the rain. —*plural* **um·brel′ las**

un·a·ble (un ā′b′l) *adjective*   not having the power to do something [We were *unable* to push the car.]

un·a·fraid (un ə frād′) *adjective*   not feeling fear.

un·bro·ken (un brō′ k′n) *adjective*   not broken.

un·but·ton (un but′ ′n) *verb*   to unfasten the buttons of. —**un·but′ toned, un·but′ ton·ing**

un·cle (uŋ′ k′l) *noun*   the brother of one's father or mother. —*plural* **un′ cles**

un·cov·er (un kuv′ ər) *verb*   to remove the cover from [*Uncover* the bird cage.] —**un·cov′ ered, un·cov′ er·ing**

un·der (un′ dər) *preposition*   in a lower position; below [It rolled *under* the table.]

un·der·stand (un dər stand′) *verb*   to get the meaning of [Do you *understand* my question?] —**un·der·stood′, un·der·stand′ ing**

un·e·qual (un ē′ kwəl) *adjective*   not equal [We were given *unequal* shares.]

un·e·ven (un ē′ vən) *adjective*   not even [Be careful on the *uneven* ground.]

un·fair (un fer′) *adjective*   not fair or honest [The umpire's call was *unfair*.]

un·fas·ten (un fas′ ′n) *verb*   untie; open, etc. —**un·fas′ tened, un·fas′ ten·ing**

un·health·y (un hel′ thē) *adjective*   not well; sick. —**un·health′ i·er, un·health′ i·est**

un·hurt (un hurt′) *adjective* not having pain, injury, or harm [She came out of the burning building *unhurt*.]

un·kind (un kīnd′) *adjective* not kind; hurting the feelings of others [Those *unkind* words made him sad.]

un·less (ən les′) *conjunction* except if [I won't go *unless* you do.]

un·lock (un läk′) *verb* to open by undoing a lock [This key won't *unlock* the door.] —**un·locked′, un·lock′ ing**

un·o·pened (un ō′ p'nd) *adjective* closed or covered [What was behind the *unopened* door?]

un·pack (un pak′) *verb* to open and empty out [I'll *unpack* the suitcase.] —**un·packed′, un·pack· ing**

un·plug (un plug′) *verb* to remove a plug. —**un·plugged′, un·plug′ ging**

un·ripe (un rīp′) *adjective* not ripe [Don't eat the *unripe* fruit.]

un·safe (un sāf′) *adjective* not safe; dangerous [That shaky ladder is *unsafe*.]

un·tie (un tī′) *verb* to unfasten something that is tied. —**un·tied′, un·ty′ ing**

un·true (un trōo′) *adjective* not correct; false [What he said was *untrue*.]

un·will·ing (un wil′ ing) *adjective* not willing or ready [He is *unwilling* to take the blame.]

un·wise (un wīz′) *adjective* not showing good sense [It's *unwise* to skate without knee pads.]

un·wrap (un rap′) *verb* to open by taking off the wrapping. —**un·wrapped′, un·wrap′ ping**

up·stairs (up′ sterz′) *adverb* to or on an upper floor [Let's go *upstairs*.]

use (yōoz) *verb* to put into action [He *used* the vacuum cleaner.] —**used, us′ ing**

V

val·ley (val′ ē) *noun* low land between hills or mountains. —*plural* **val′ leys**

vase (vās *or* vāz) *noun* a container for holding flowers. —*plural* **vas′ es**

ver·y (ver′ ē) *adverb* extremely [It is *very* cold.]

view (vyōo) *noun* scene [We admired the *view* from the bridge.] —*plural* **views**

W

wade (wād) *verb* to walk through water, mud, or anything that slows one down. —**wad′ ed, wad′ ing**

wag (wag) *verb* to move quickly back and forth [The dog *wagged* its tail.] —**wagged, wag′ ging**

wag·on (wag′ ən) *noun* a four-wheeled vehicle for carrying heavy loads [Two horses pulled the *wagon*.] —*plural* **wag′ ons**

wake (wāk) *verb* awake [*Wake* up!] —**woke, wak′ ing**

walk (wôk) *verb* to move along on foot [*Walk*, do not run, to the nearest exit.] **walked, walk′ ing**

warm (wôrm) *adjective* having or feeling a little heat; not cool but not hot [I was too *warm*, so I took off my sweater.]

warn (wôrn) *verb* to tell of danger [The lighthouse beamed a signal to *warn* ships.] —**warned, warn′ ing**

was·n't (wuz′ 'nt) was not.

watch (wäch *or* wôch) *verb* to look at [They *watched* the parade.] —**watched, watch′ ing**

water (wôt′ ər) *noun* the liquid that falls as rain and is found in lakes, rivers, and oceans.

a	fat	ir	here	ou	out	zh	leisure
ā	ape	ī	bite, fire	u	up	ng	ring
ä	car, lot	ō	go	ur	fur		a *in* ago
e	ten	ô	law, horn	ch	chin		e *in* agent
er	care	oi	oil	sh	she	ə =	i *in* unity
ē	even	oo	look	th	thin		o *in* collect
i	hit	ōo	tool	th	then		u *in* focus

wave (wāv) *verb*　to move back and forth [The toddler *waved* his hand.] —**waved, wav′ ing**

wear (wer) *verb*　to have on the body [Do you *wear* glasses?] —**wore, worn, wear′ ing**

weath·er (weth′ ər) *noun*　the conditions outside relating to temperature, sunshine, etc. [We have good *weather* today for a picnic.]

we'd (wēd)　**1** we had.　**2** we should.　**3** we would.

week·end (wēk′ end′) *noun*　the time from Friday night to Monday morning. —*plural* **week′ ends′**

we'll (wēl) we will.

we're (wir) we are.

weren't (wʉrnt) were not.

wet (wet) *adjective*　covered or soaked with liquid [Wipe it off with a *wet* rag.] —**wet′ ter, wet′ test**

what's (hwuts) what is.

who's (hōōz) who is, who has.

wide (wīd) *adjective*　measuring a lot from side to side [The trailer was very *wide*.] —**wid′ er, wid′ est**

wife (wīf) *noun*　a married woman. —*plural* **wives**

wig·gle (wig′ 'l) *verb*　to twist from side to side [The polliwog moves by *wiggling* its tail.] —**wig′ gled, wig′ gling**

will·ing (wil′ ing) *adjective*　agreeing to do something [Are you *willing* to try?]

win (win) *verb*　to get the victory in a contest [I might *win* the spelling bee.] —**won, win′ ning**

wind·y (win′ dē) *adjective*　with much wind [It's a *windy* day.] —**wind′ i·er, wind′ i·est**

win·ner (win′ ər) *noun*　one that wins a contest or race [The *winner* of the election will be president.] —*plural* **win′ ners**

win·ter (win′ tər) *noun*　the coldest season of the year. —*plural* **win′ ters**

wip·er (wīp′ ər) *noun*　one who wipes. —*plural* **wip′ ers**

wish (wish) *noun*　something wanted or hoped for [He got his *wish*.] —*plural* **wish′ es**

wolf (woolf) *noun*　a wild animal that looks like a dog. —*plural* **wolves**

wom·an (wōōm′ ən) *noun*　an adult female human being. —*plural* **wom′ en**

wool·en (wool′ ən) *adjective*　made of wool [He wore a heavy *woolen* jacket.]

word (wʉrd) *noun*　a sound or group of sounds having meaning and used as a single unit of speech. —*plural* **words**

work·er (wʉr′ kər) *noun*　a person who works. —*plural* **work·ers**

world (wʉrld) *noun*　the earth or a planet thought of as like the earth [Magellan's crew sailed around the *world*.] —*plural* **worlds**

worm (wʉrm) *noun*　a small, creeping animal with a soft, thin body and no legs. —*plural* **worms**

wor·ry (wʉr′ ē) *verb*　to be or make troubled in mind [She *worried* about her grades.] —**wor′ ried, wor′ ry·ing**

worst (wʉrst) *adjective*　most evil.

worth (wʉrth) *adjective*　equal in value to [It's not *worth* a nickel.]

wrap·per (rap′ ər) *noun*　a covering [Our newspaper is mailed in a paper *wrapper*.] —*plural* **wrap′ pers**

wreck (rek) *verb*　to destroy or ruin [The car was *wrecked* in an accident.] —**wrecked, wreck′ ing**

wren (ren) *noun*　a small songbird. —*plural* **wrens**

wrench (rench) *noun*   a tool for holding and turning nuts and bolts. —*plural* **wrench' es**

wrin·kle (ring' k'l) *noun*   a small or uneven fold [Can you iron the *wrinkles* from this shirt?] —*plural* **wrink' les**

wrist (rist) *noun*   the part of the arm between the hand and forearm. —*plural* **wrists**

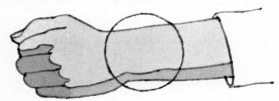

write (rīt) *verb*   to be the author of [Dickens *wrote* novels.] —**wrote, writ' ing**

wrong (rông) *adjective*   not the one that is correct or wanted [That is the *wrong* door.] ♦ *adverb* incorrectly [You answered the question *wrong*.]

Y

year (yir) *noun*   a period of 365 days. —*plural* **years**

yes·ter·day (yes' tər dē *or* yes' tər dā) *noun*   the day before today.

you'd (yo̅o̅d)   **1** you had.   **2** you would.

young (yung) *adjective*   not old [That *young* boy is very talkative.] —**young' er, young' est**

your·self (yər self') *pronoun*   your own self [Did you cut *yourself*?] —*plural* **your·selves'**

you've (yo̅o̅v) you have.

Z

zip·per (zip' ər) *noun*   a device used to fasten two edges of cloth [His coat *zipper* is stuck.] —*plural* **zip' pers**

a	fat	**ir**	here	**ou**	out	**zh**	leisure
ā	ape	**ī**	bite, fire	**u**	up	**ng**	ring
ä	car, lot	**ō**	go	**ʉr**	fur		a *in* ago
e	ten	**ô**	law, horn	**ch**	chin		e *in* agent
er	care	**oi**	oil	**sh**	she	**ə** =	i *in* unity
ē	even	**oo**	look	**th**	thin		o *in* collect
i	hit	**o̅o̅**	tool	***th***	then		u *in* focus

Lesson 2

oa

boat
float
goat

Lesson 4

xes

boxes
foxes

Lesson 5

ys

cowboys
plays
trays
keys

Lesson 11

bb

ribbon

Lesson 13

yed

stayed
obeyed
sprayed
played

Lesson 14

wr

wrote

Lesson 16

gg

wagged
begged
bragged

or

fork

short

world

story

er

river

every

summer

dy

windy

shady

muddy

ear

wear
earth
year

igh

flight
high
light

mb

comb
crumb
lamb
climb

ck

unlock

unpack

ve

I've,

you ve

tt

little

bottle

rattle

cattle

a b c d e f g h i j k l m n

o p q r s t u v w x y z

A B C D E F G H I J K L

M N O P Q R S T U V

W X Y Z

a b c d e f g h i j

k l m n o p q r s

t u v w x y z

A B C D E F G H I

J K L M N O P Q R

S T U V W X Y Z